ISBN: 9781686029103

About the author:
Jady Alvarez is a homeschool mom of 5, content creator, and curriculum writer with over a decade of experience working with her children and other students. She strives to create content to help children thrive with simple methods she has developed that make learning engaging and enjoyable. Feel free to check her free educational video library on youtube.

Website: JadyAlvarez.Com
Youtube Educational Videos: https://www.youtube.com/c/JadyAlvarez
Instagram: JadyAHomeschool

Instructions: Have the child do the book in order as the book has a particular letter order designed to go from the easiest letters to the hardest letters. Have the child practice the one letter a day!

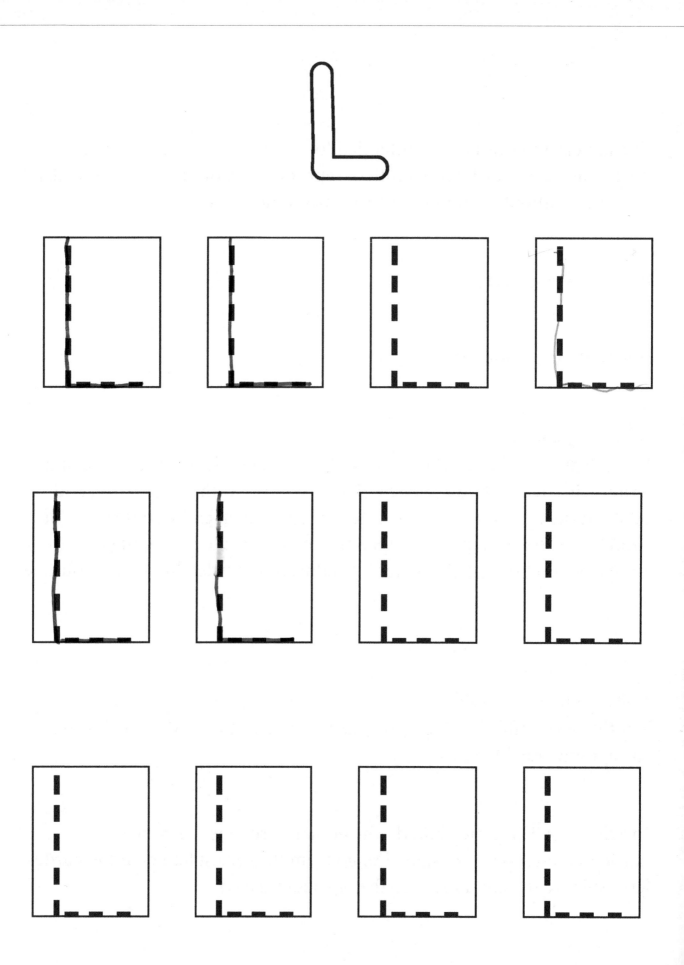

2

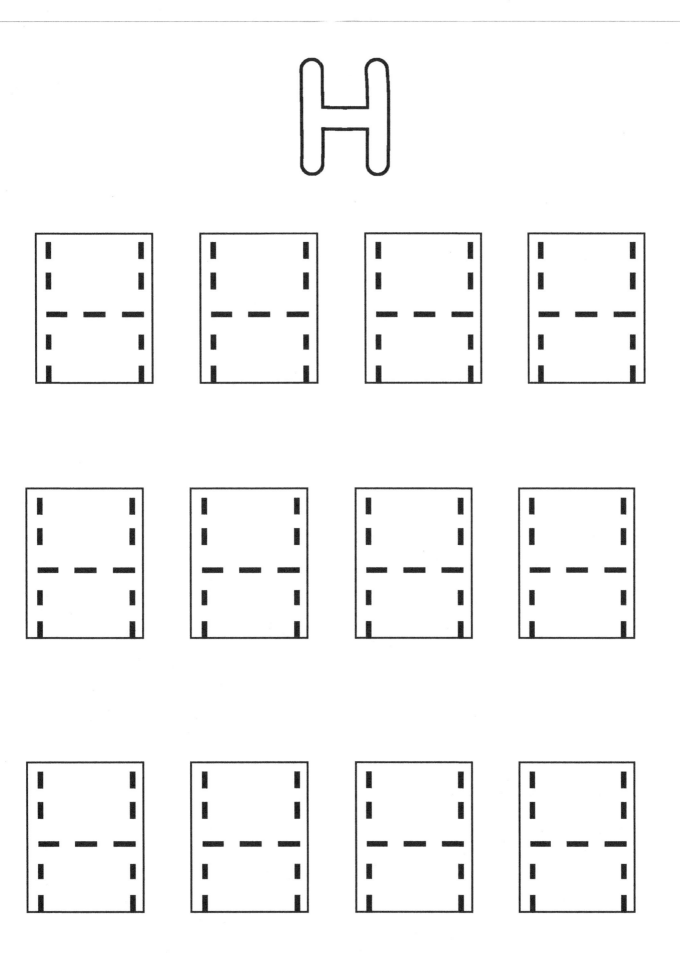

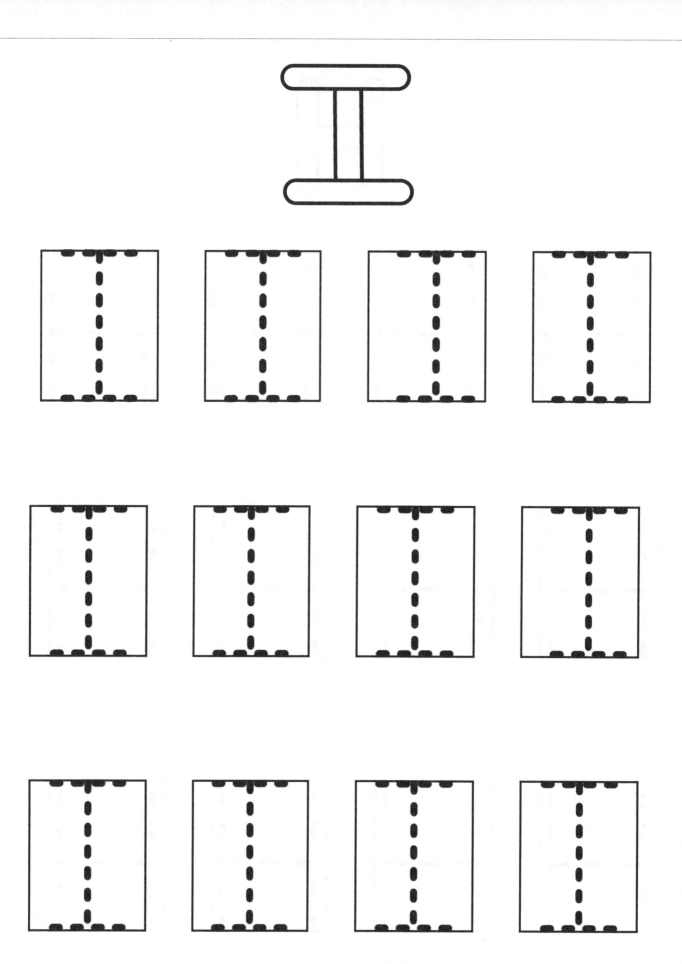

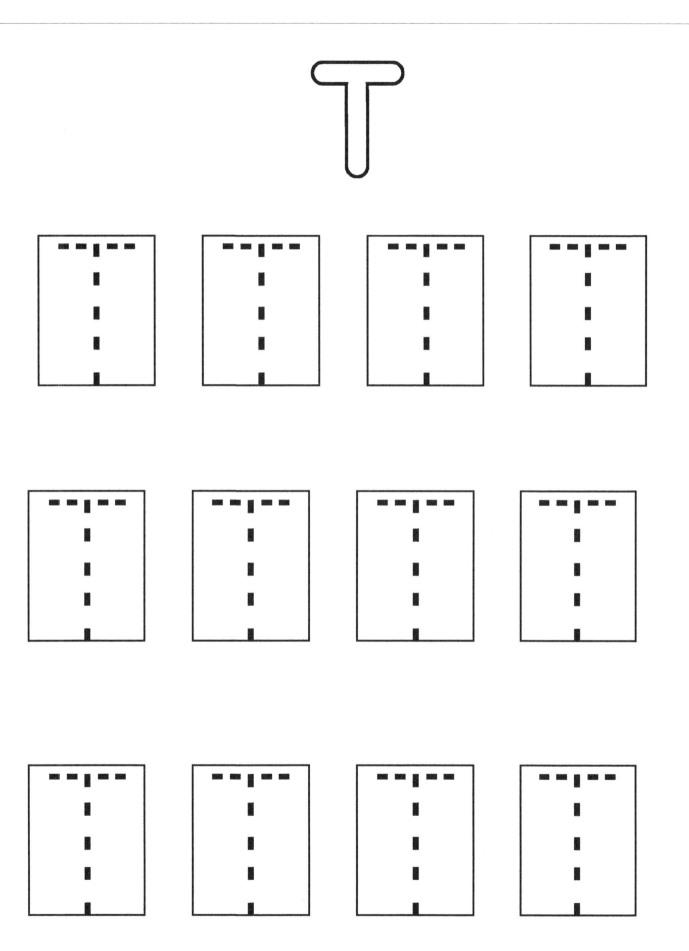

E

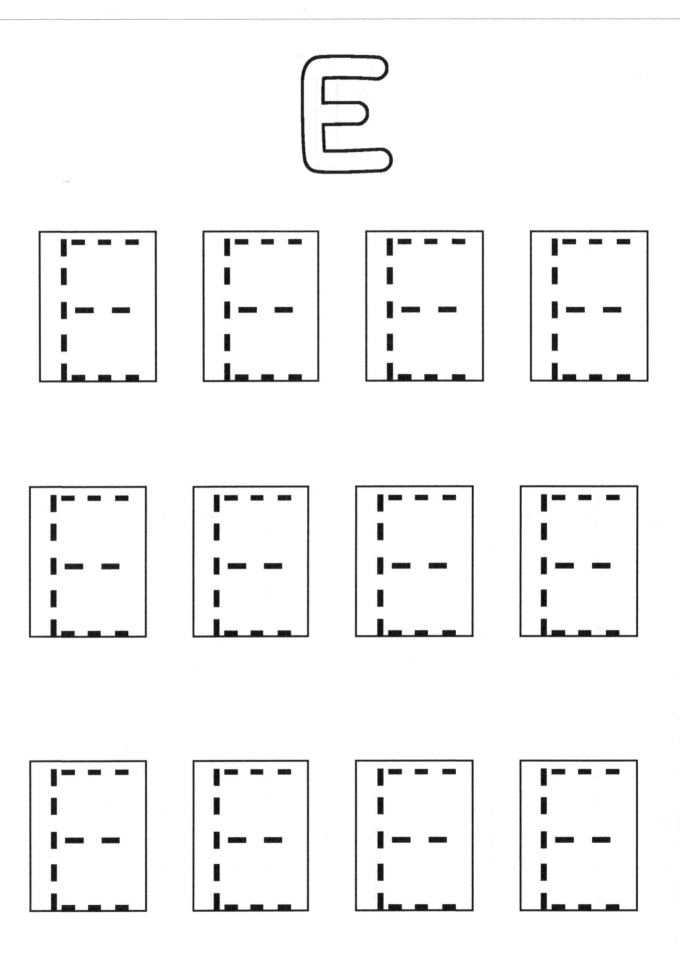

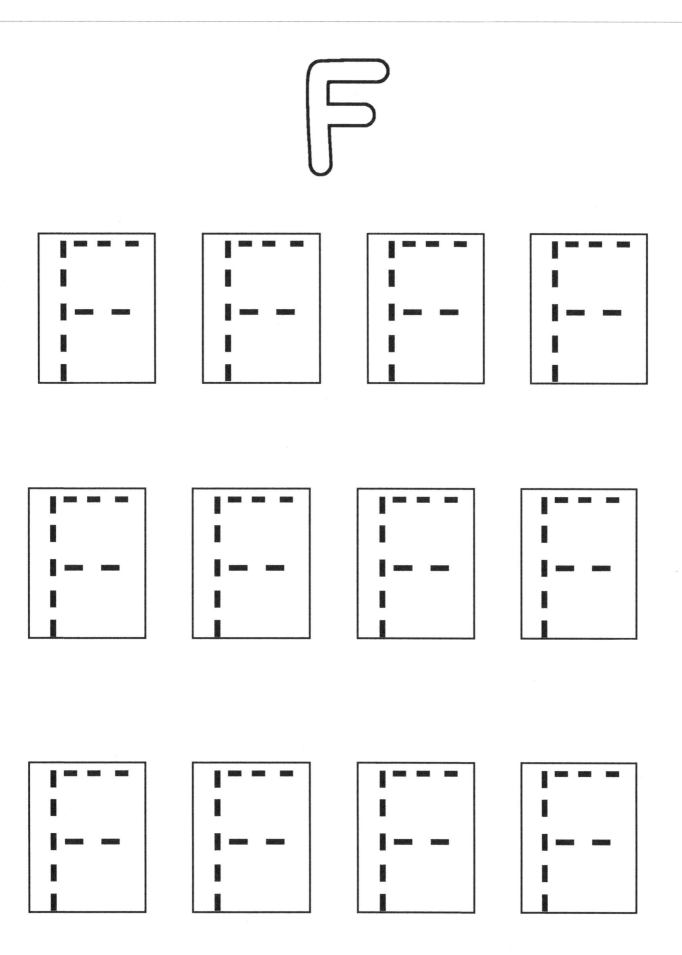

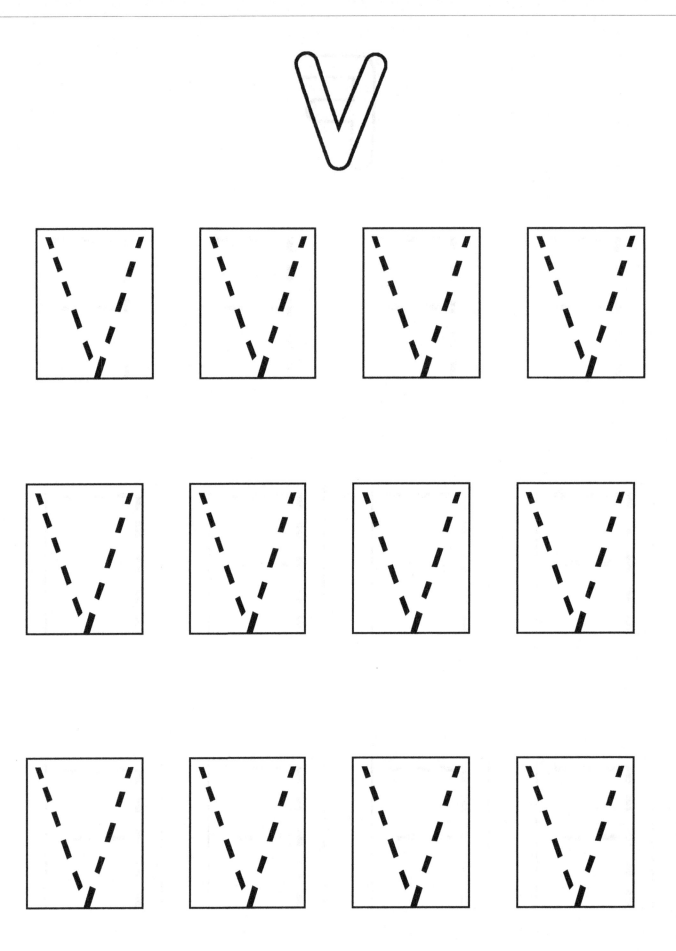

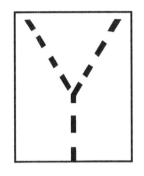  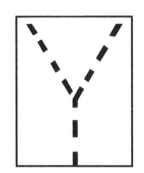 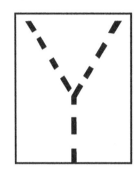

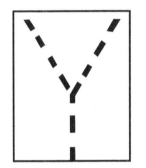 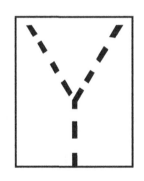 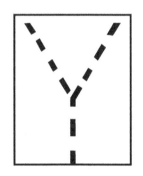 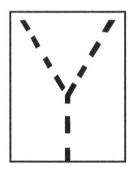

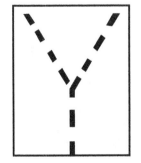 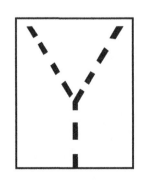 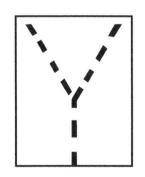 

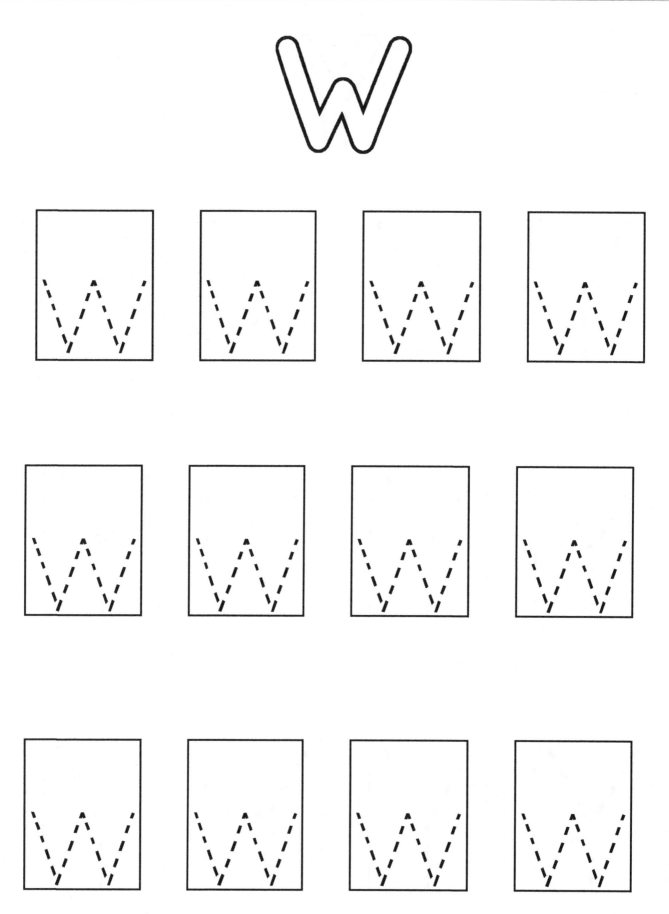

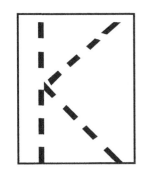 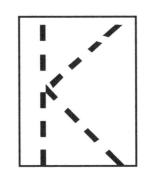 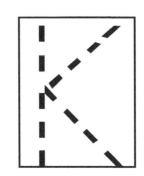 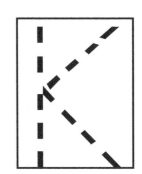

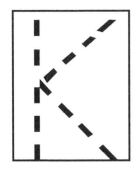 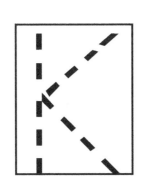 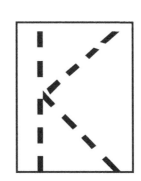 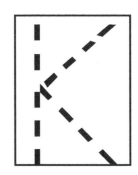

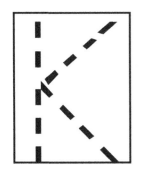 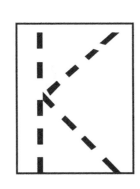 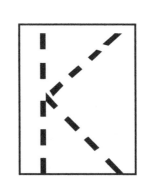 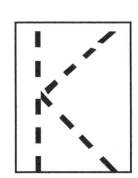

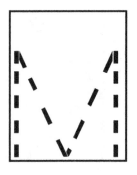 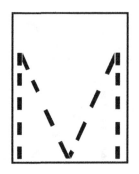 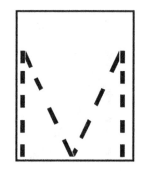 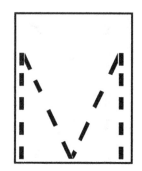

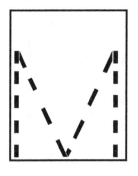  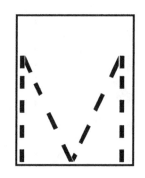 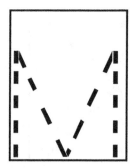

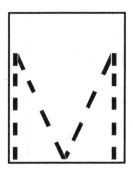 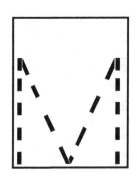 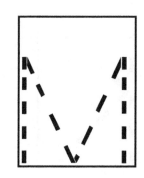 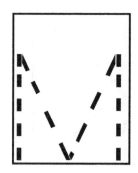

12

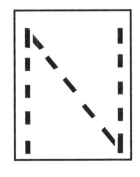 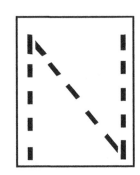 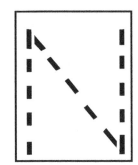 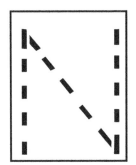

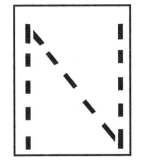 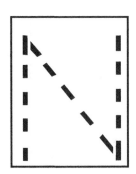 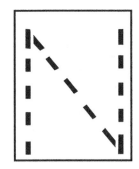 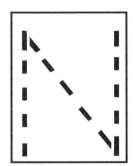

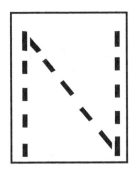 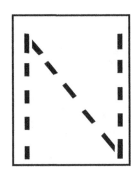 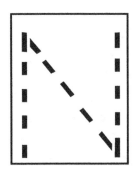 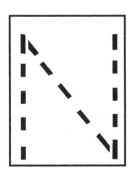

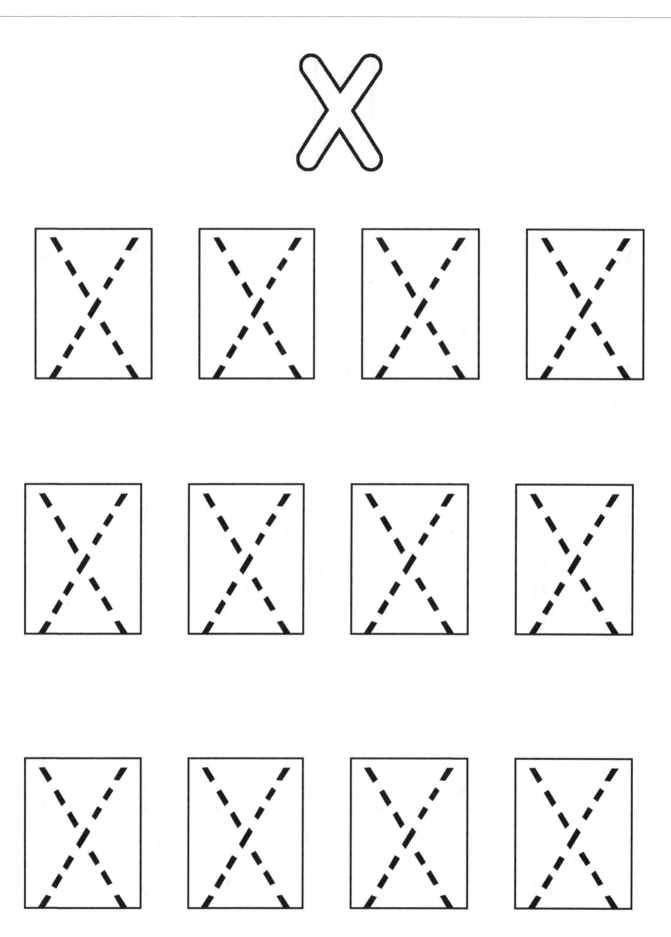

 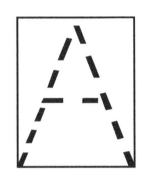 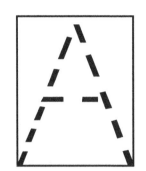 

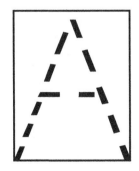 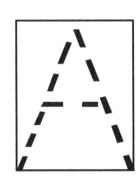 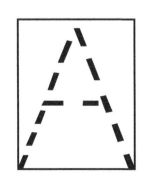 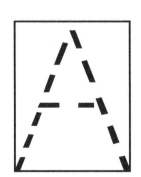

Z

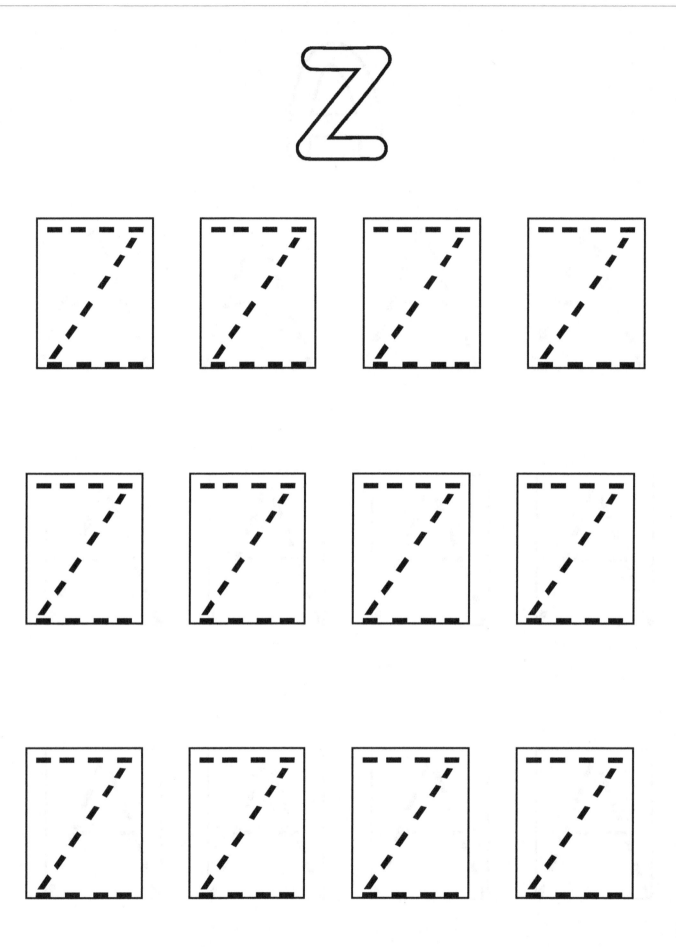

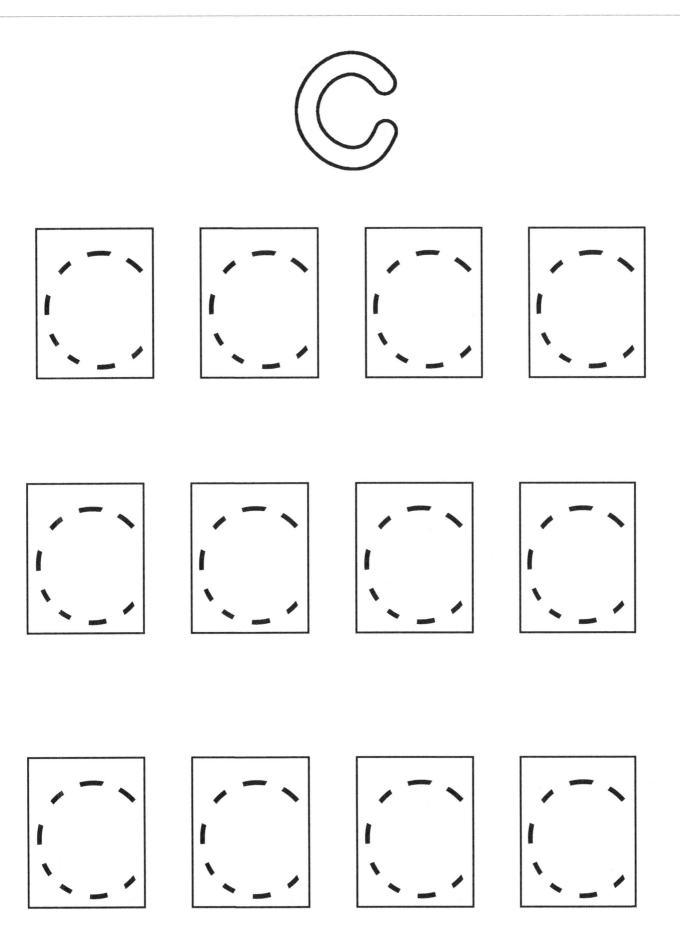

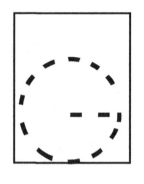 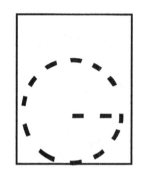 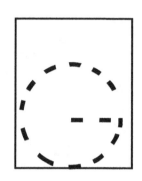 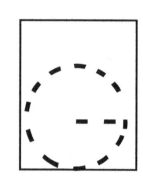

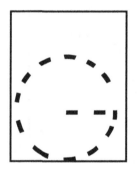 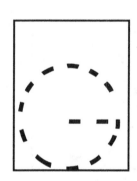 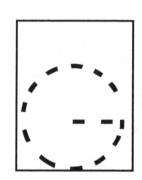 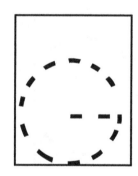

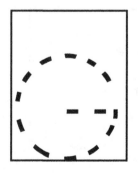 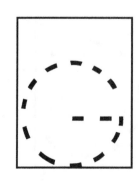 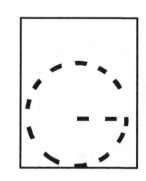 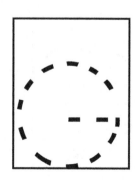

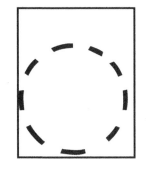 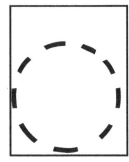 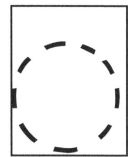 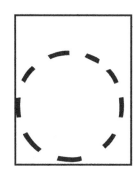

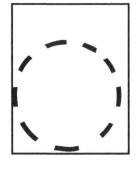 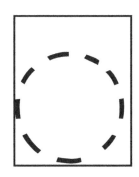 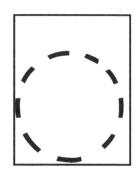 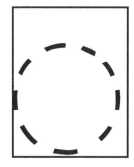

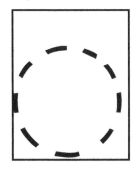 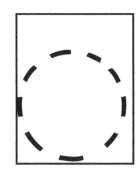 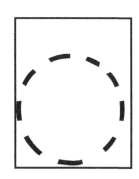 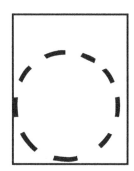

19

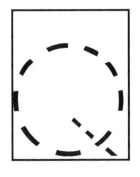 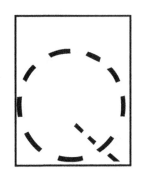 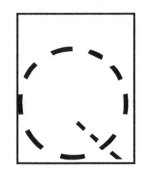 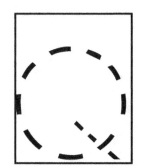

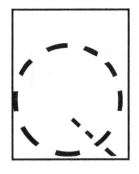 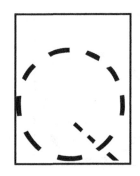 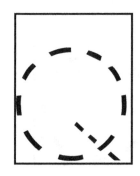 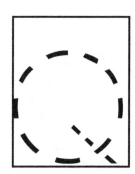

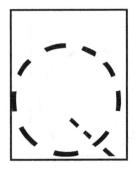 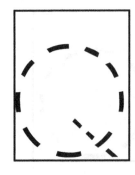 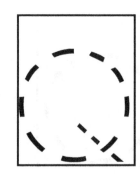 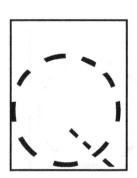

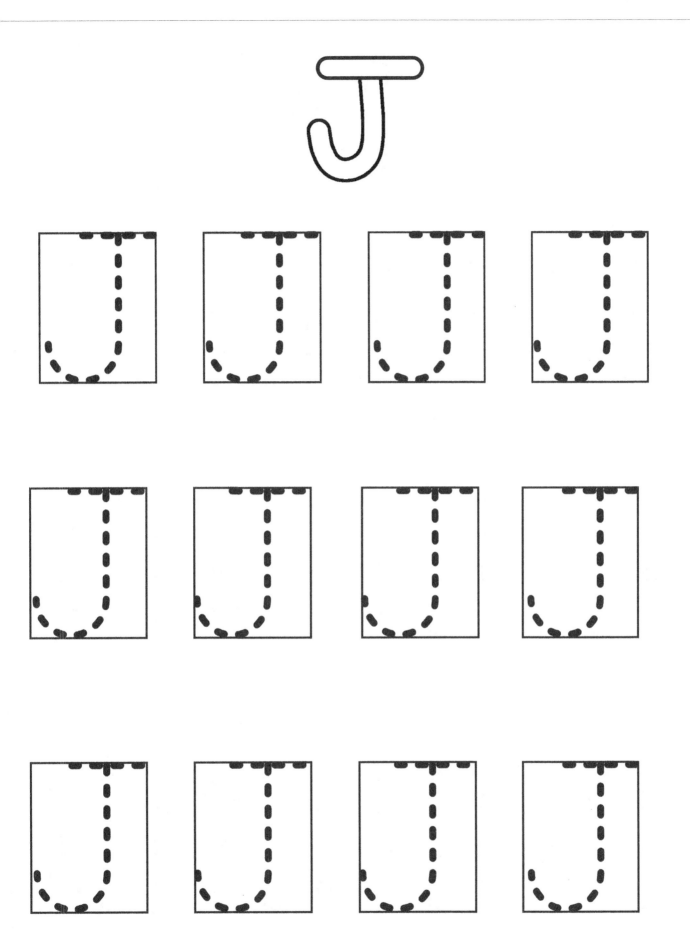

D

2

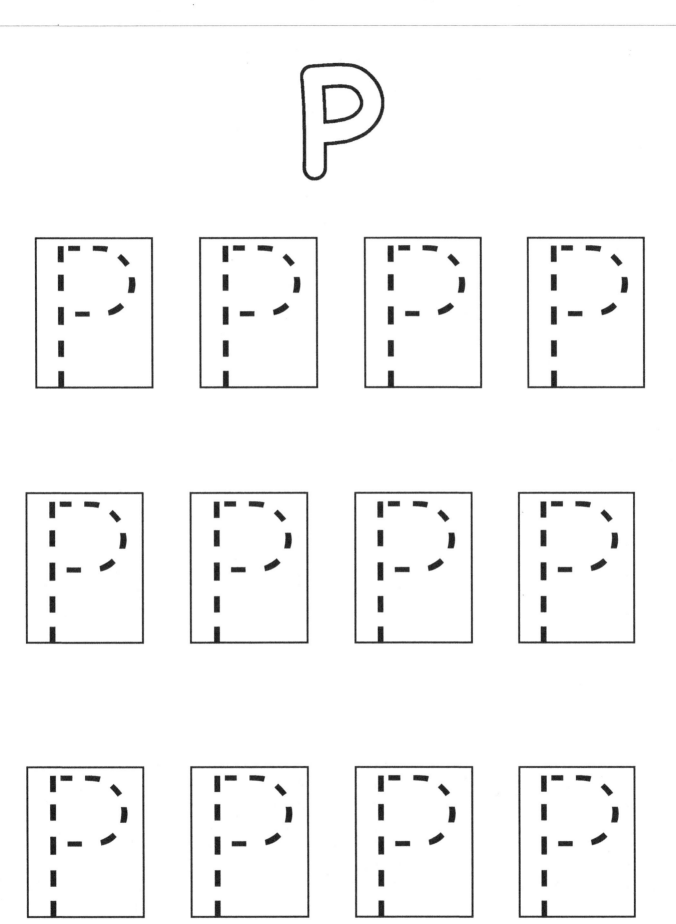

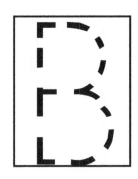 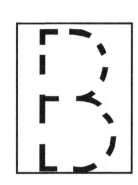 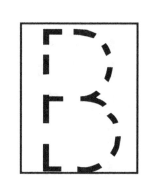 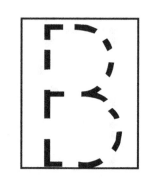

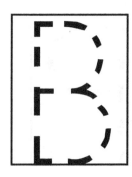 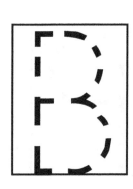 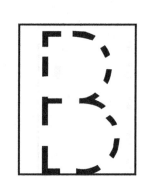 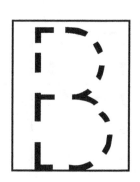

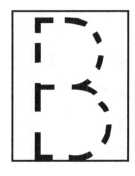 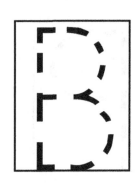 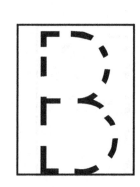 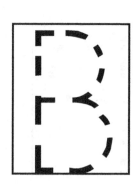

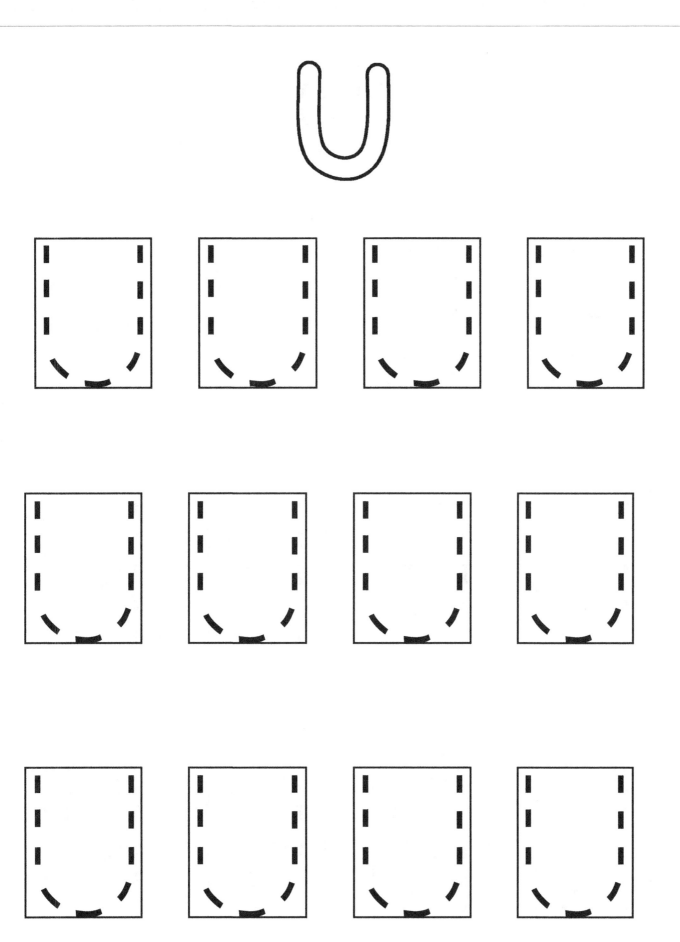

R

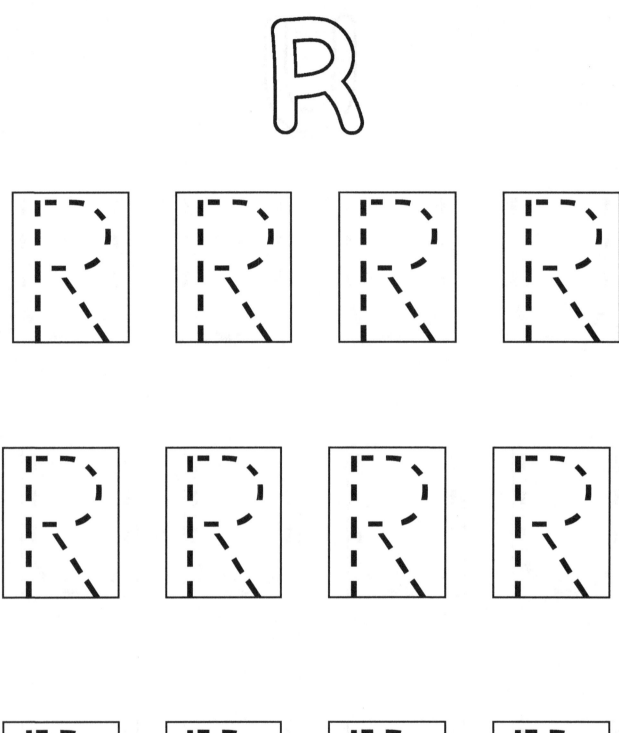

2

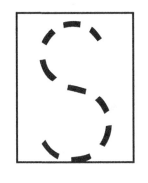 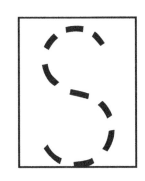 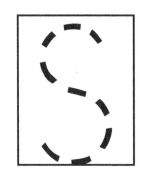 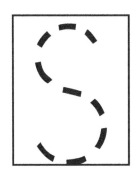

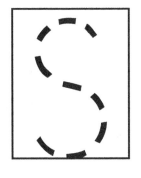 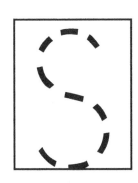 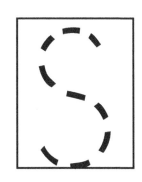 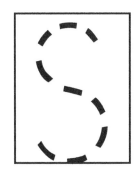

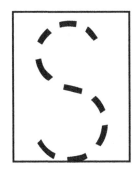 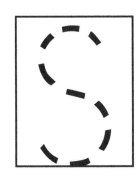 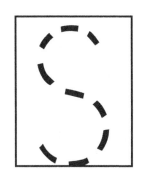 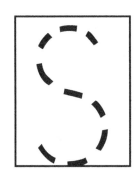

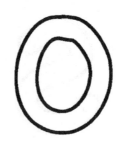

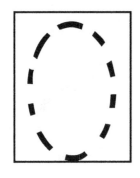 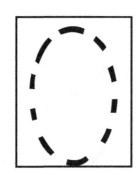 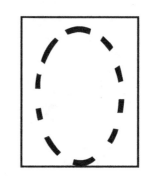 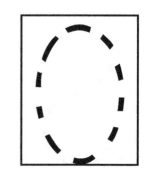

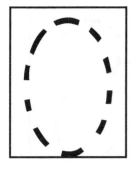 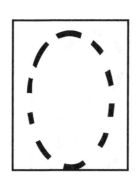 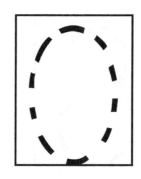 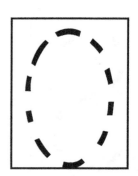

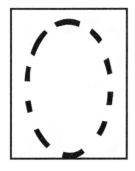 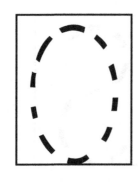 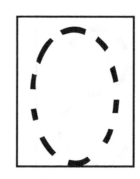 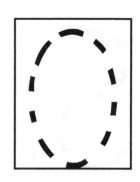

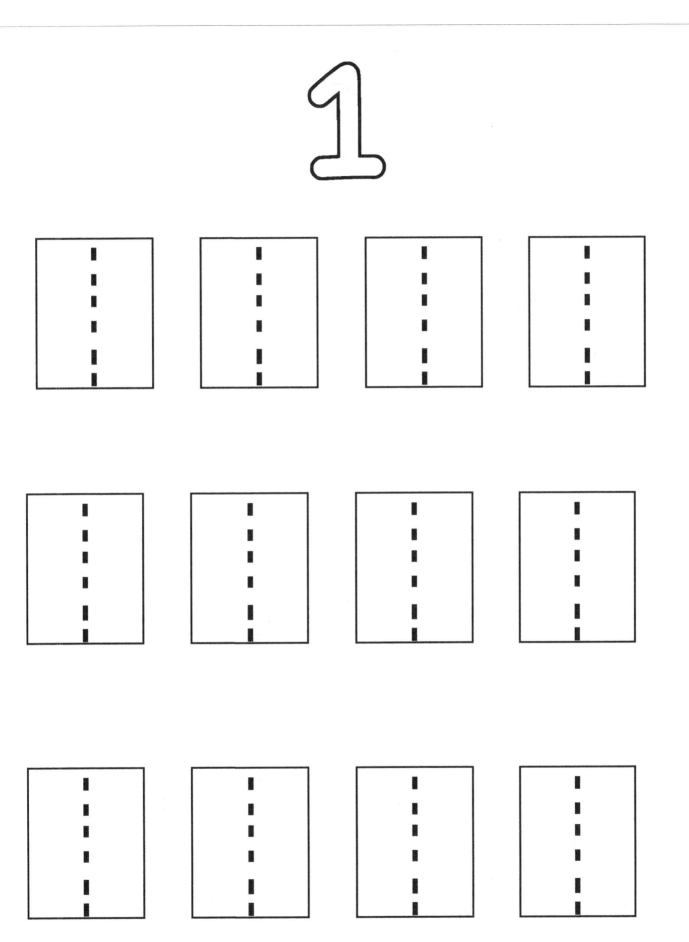

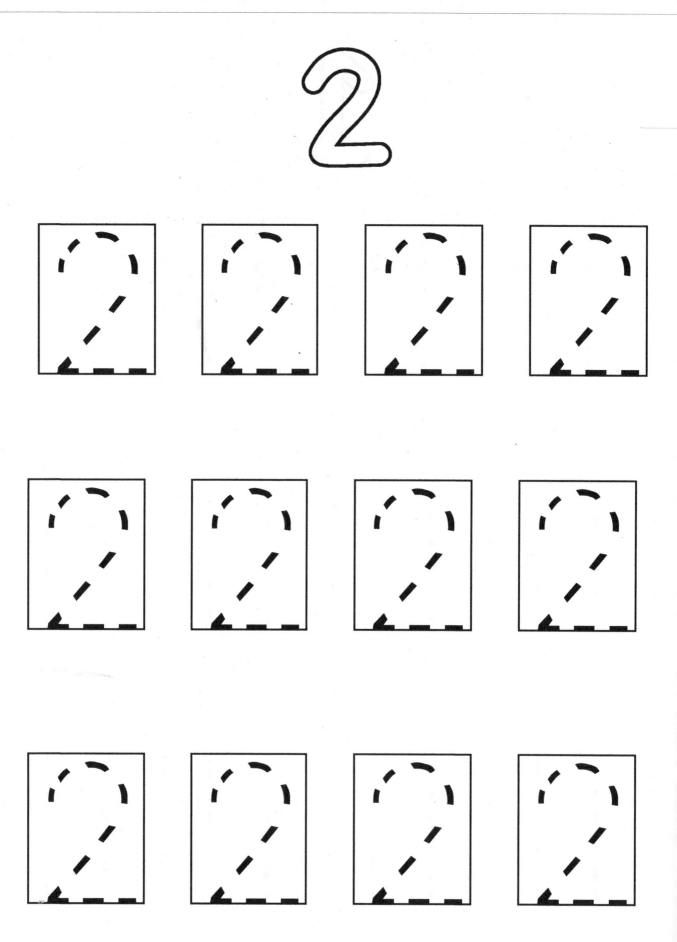

 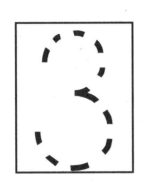 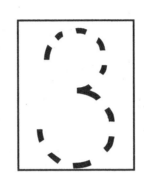 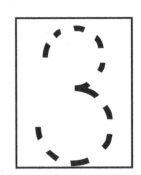

 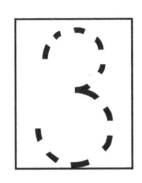 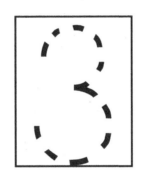 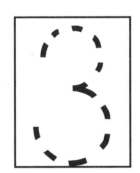

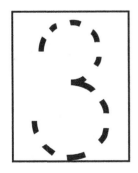 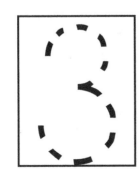 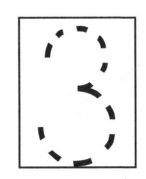 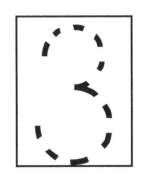

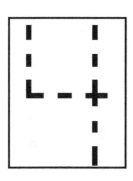 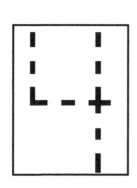 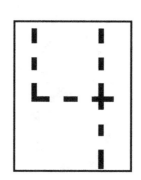 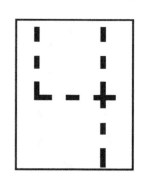

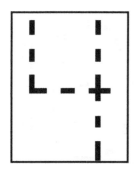 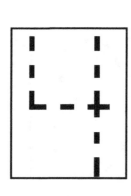 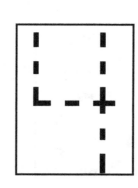 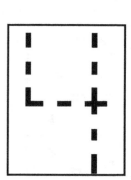

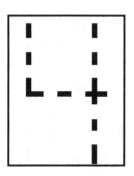 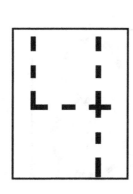 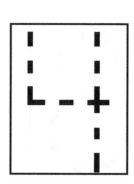 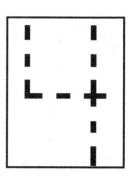

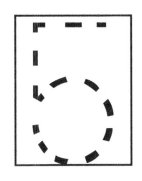 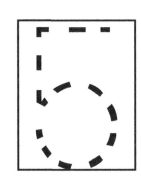 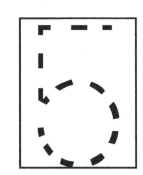 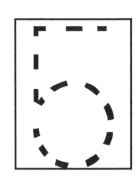

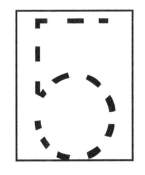 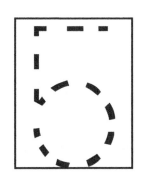 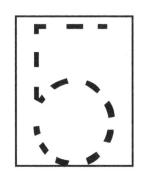 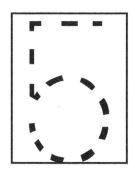

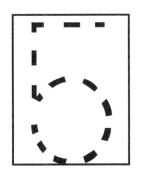 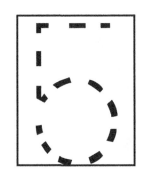 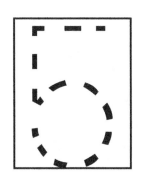 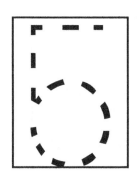

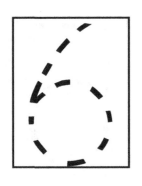  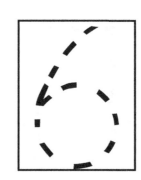 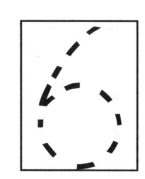

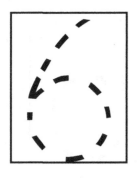 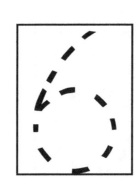 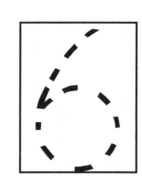 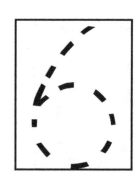

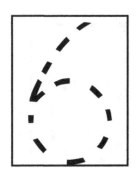 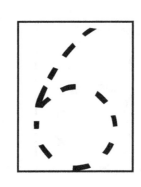 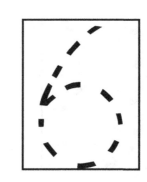 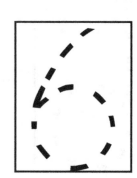

7

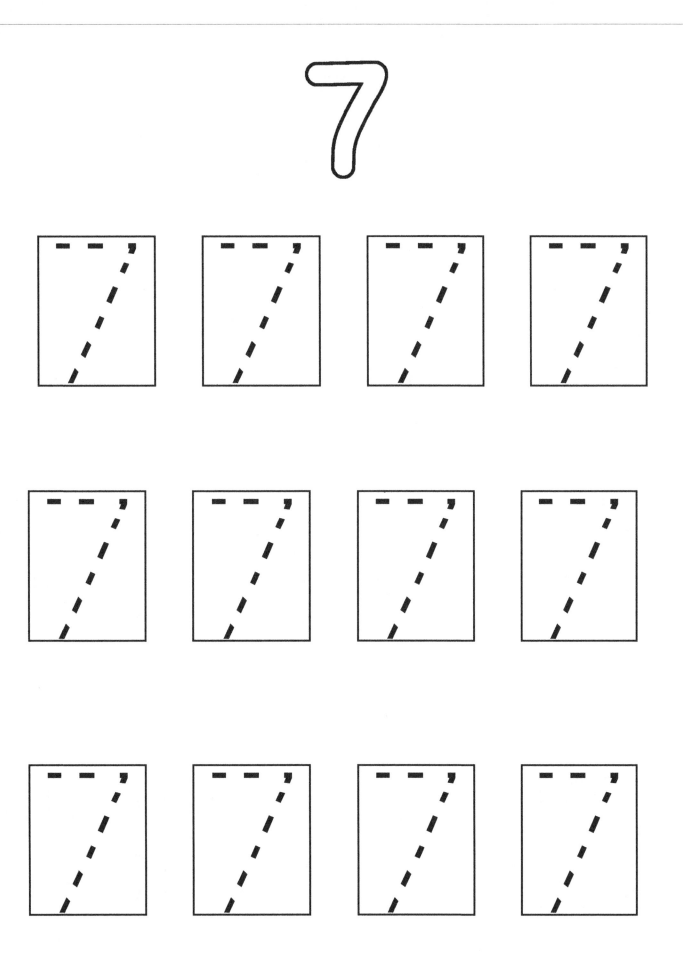

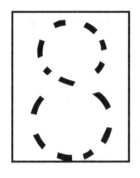 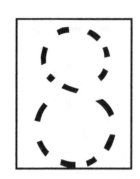 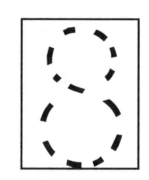 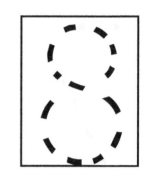

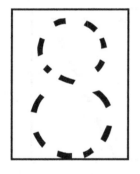 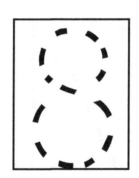 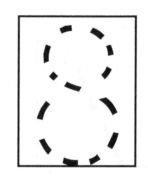 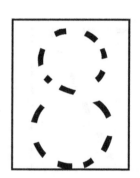

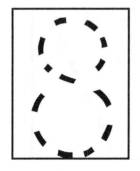 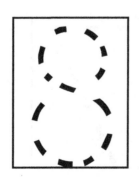 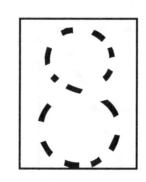 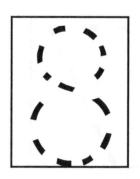

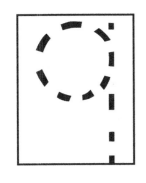 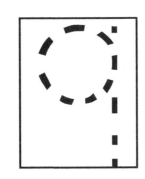 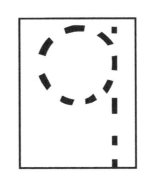 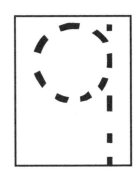

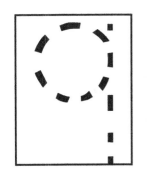 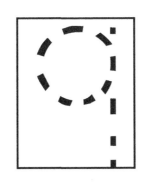 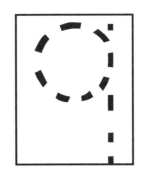 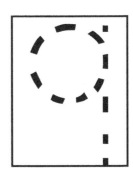

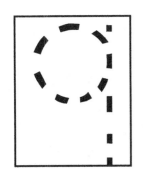 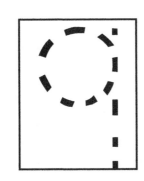 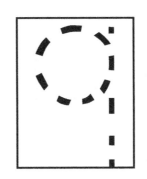 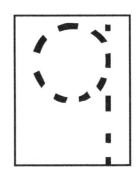

10

3

Aa

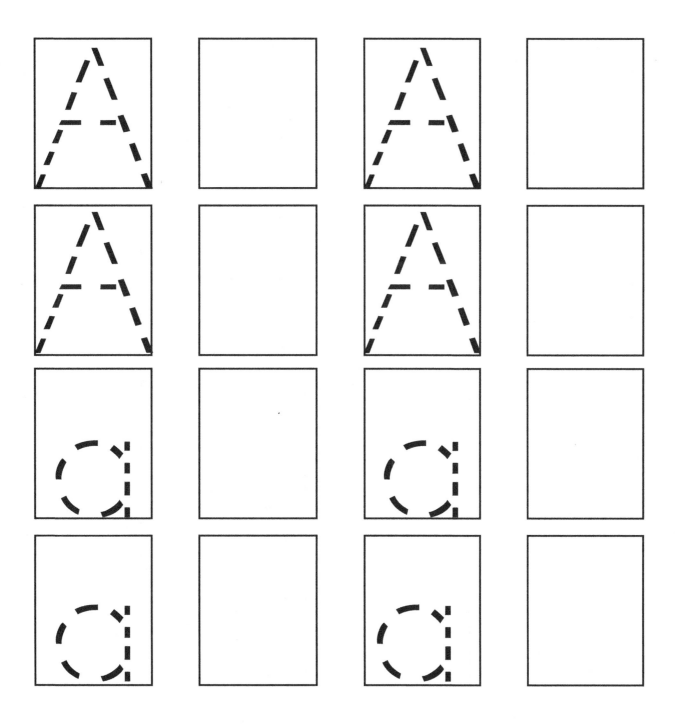

Bb

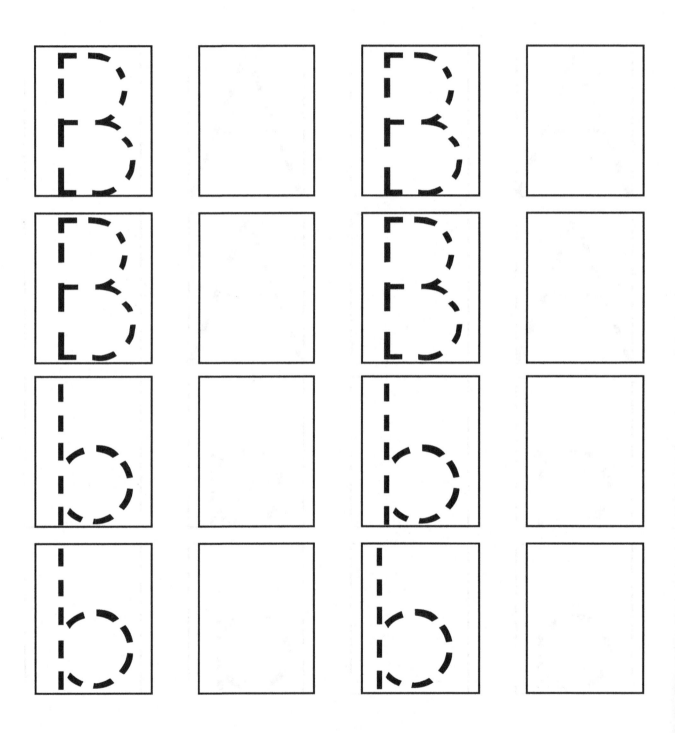

Cc

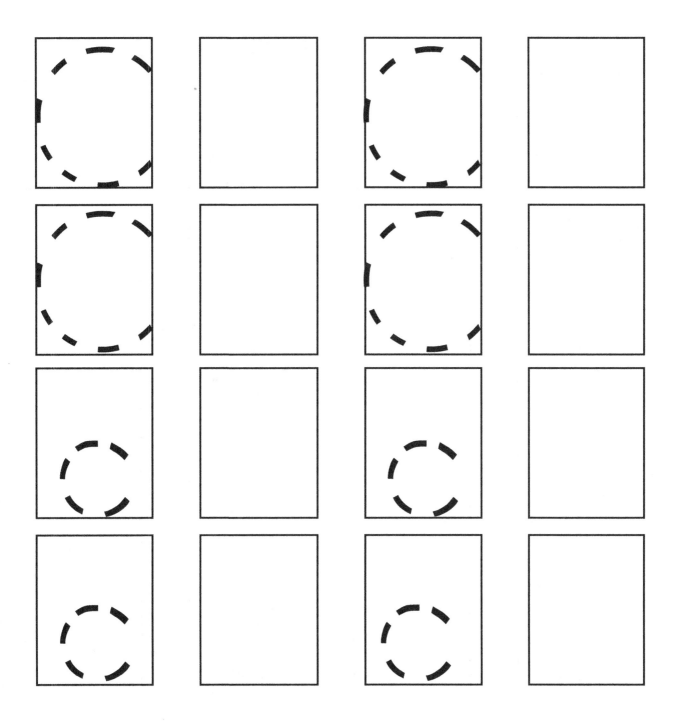

Dd

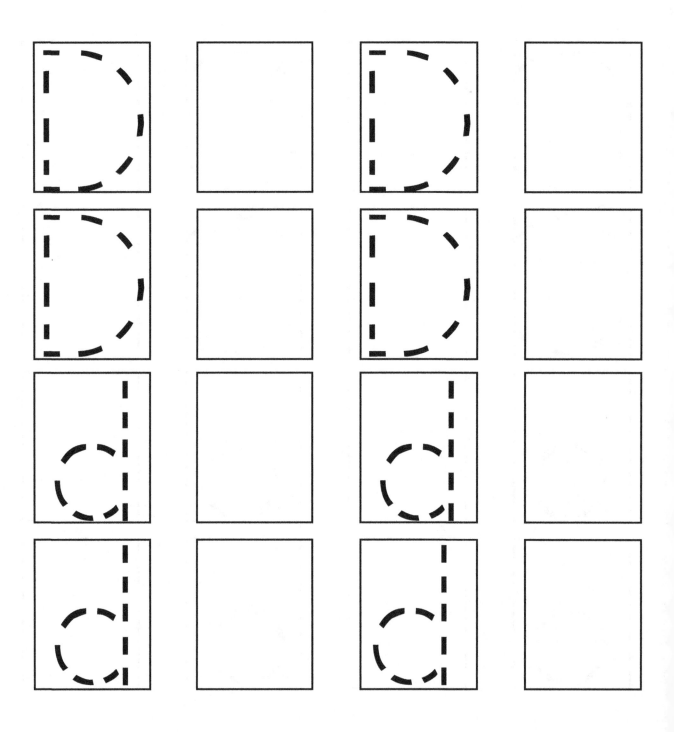

Ee

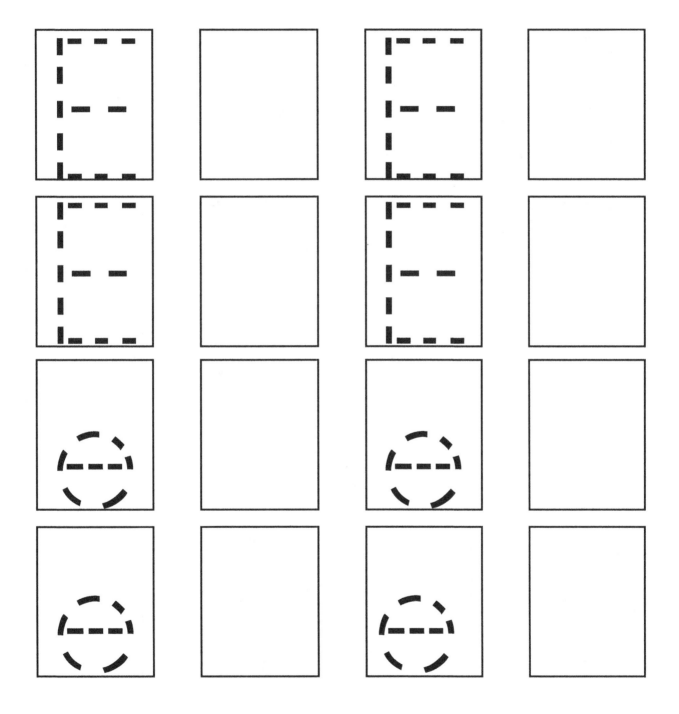

Ff

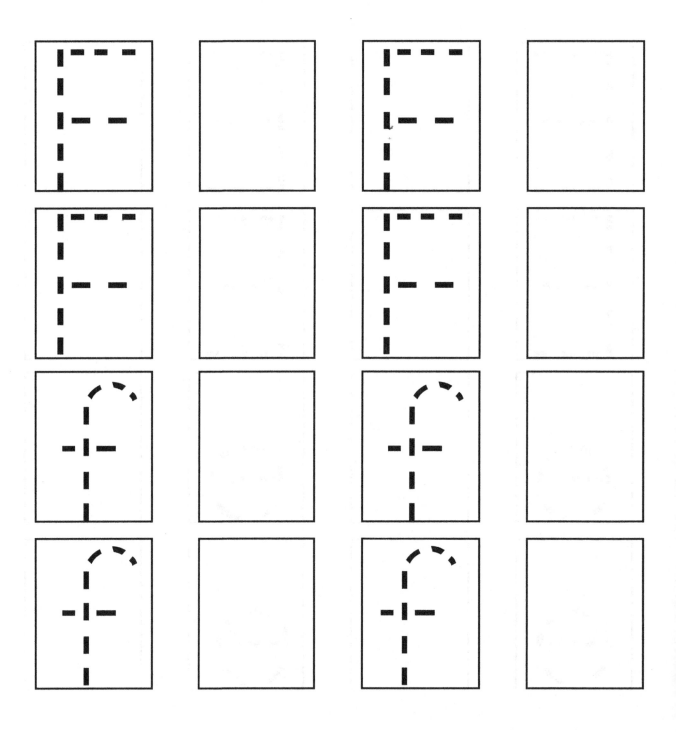

44

Gg

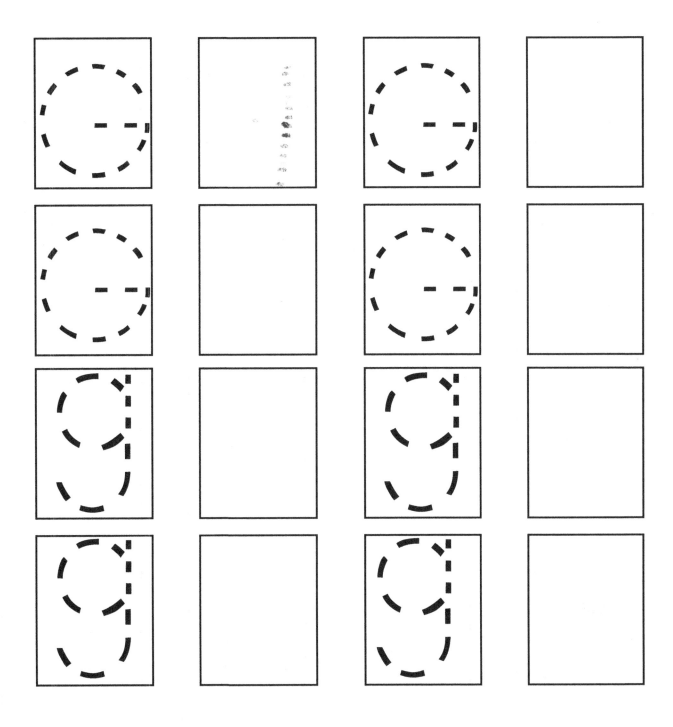

Hh

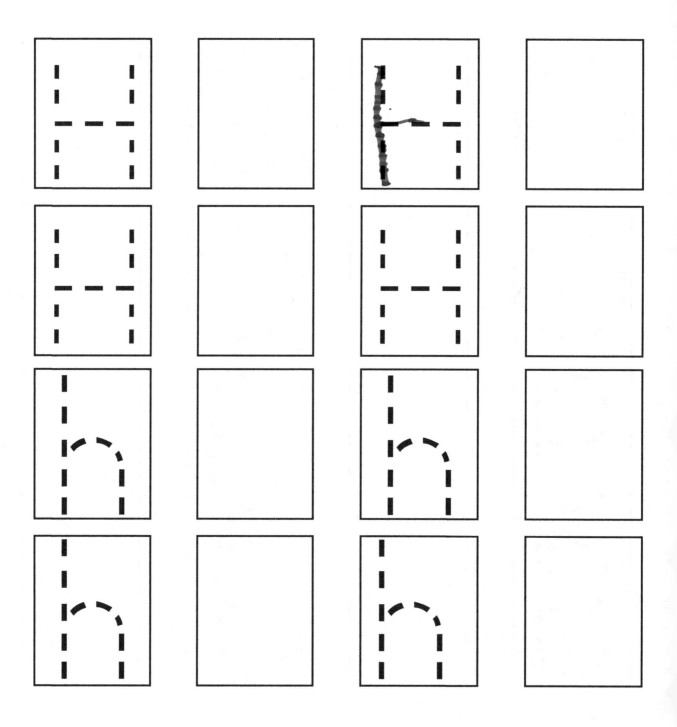

Ii

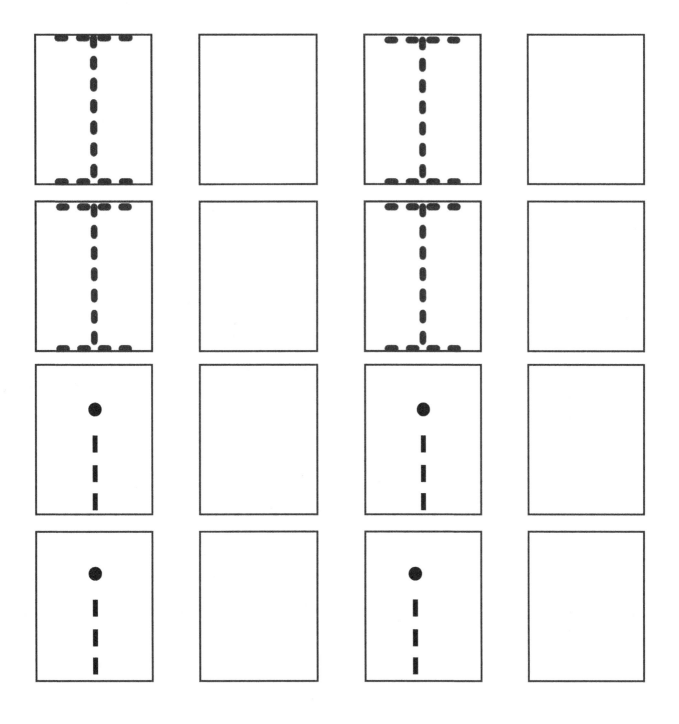

Jj

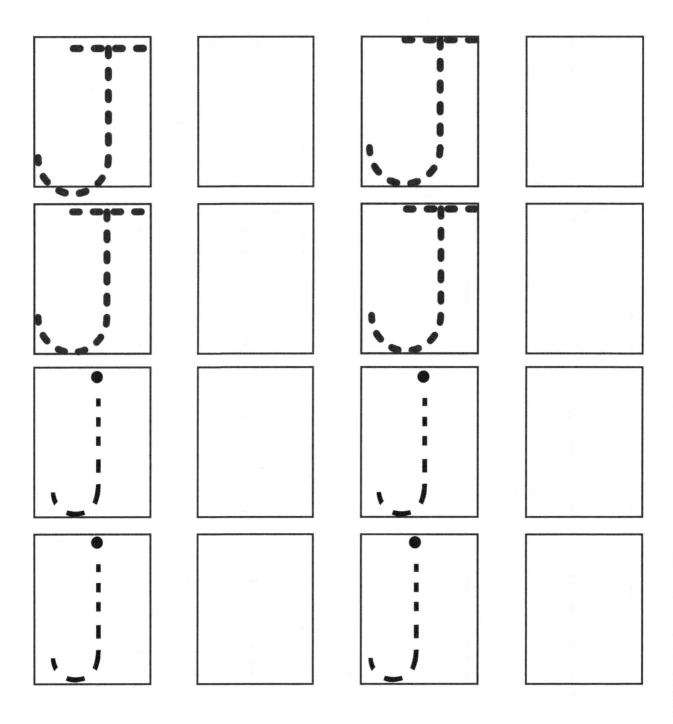

Kk

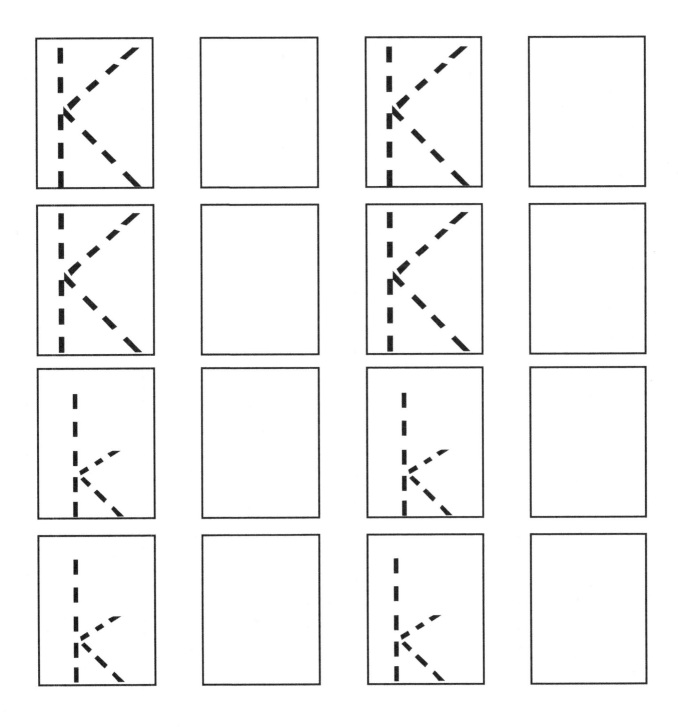

Ll

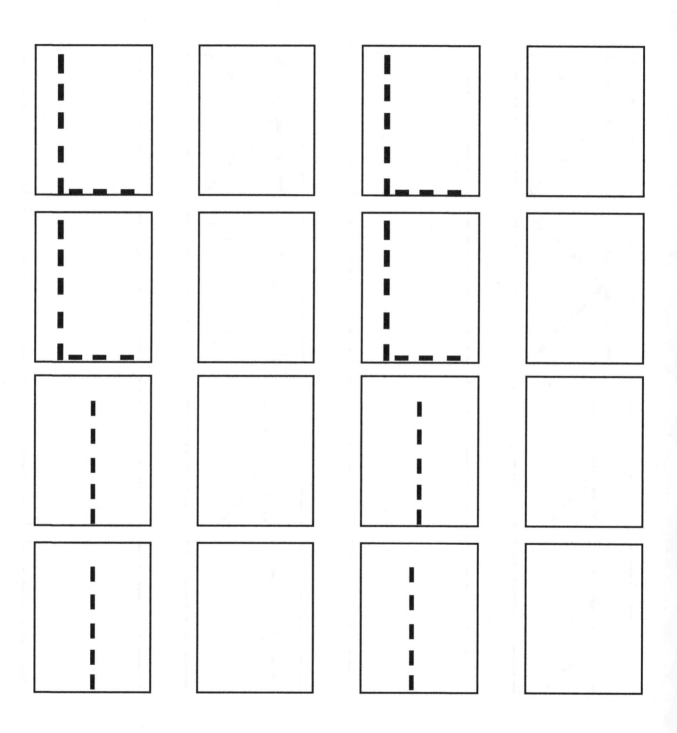

Mm

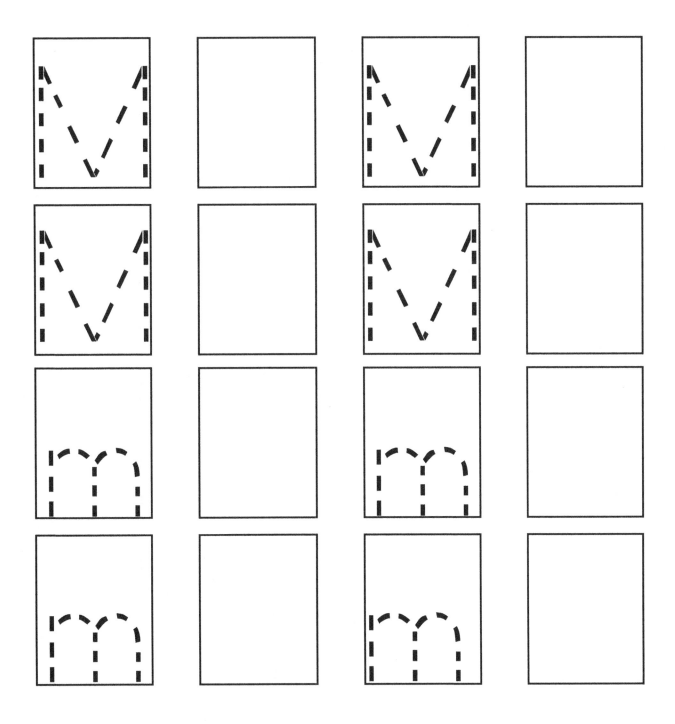

Nn

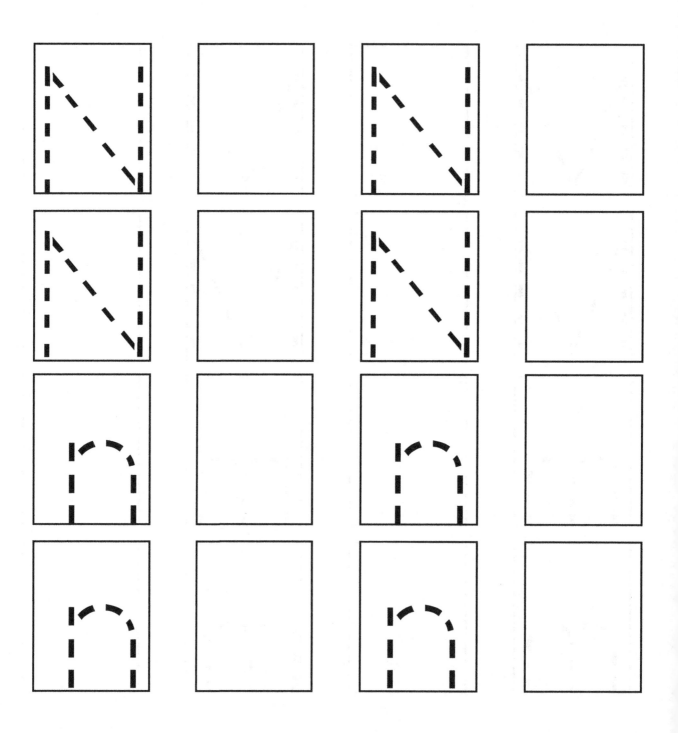

Oo

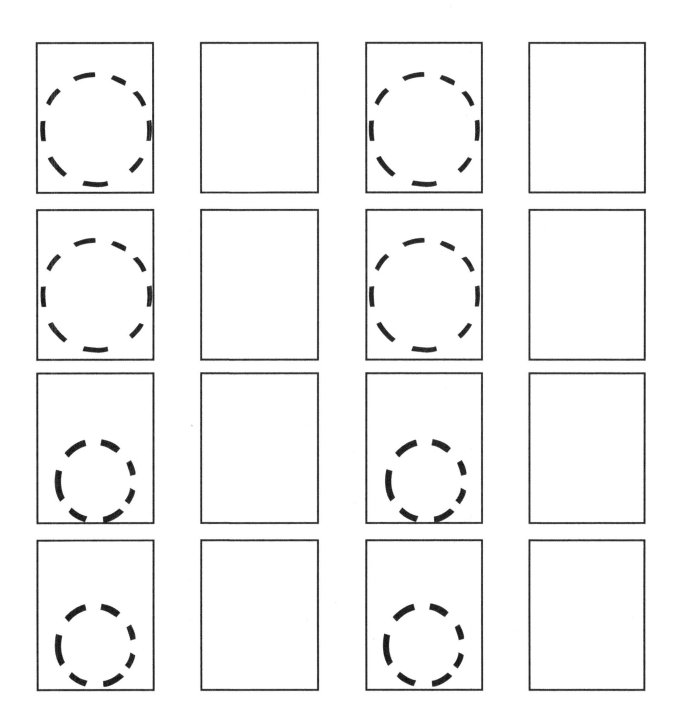

Pp

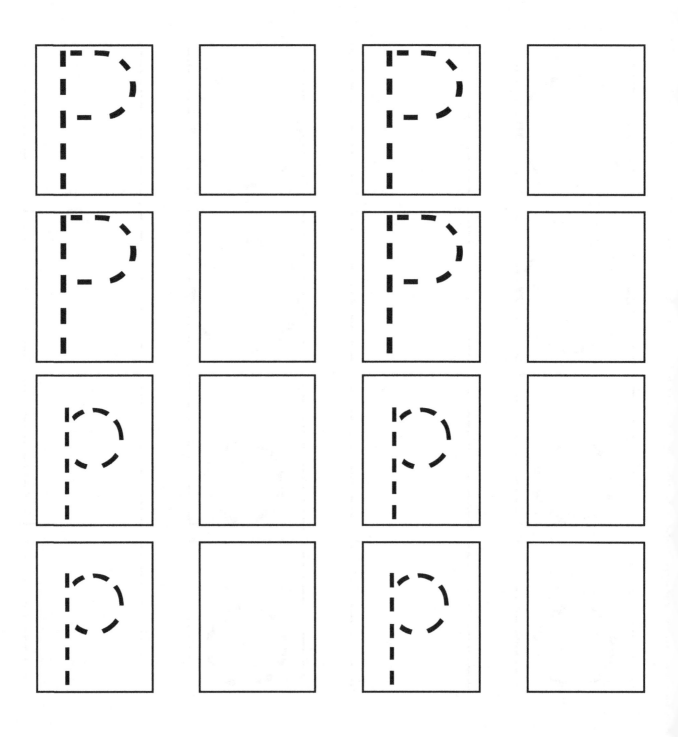

Qq

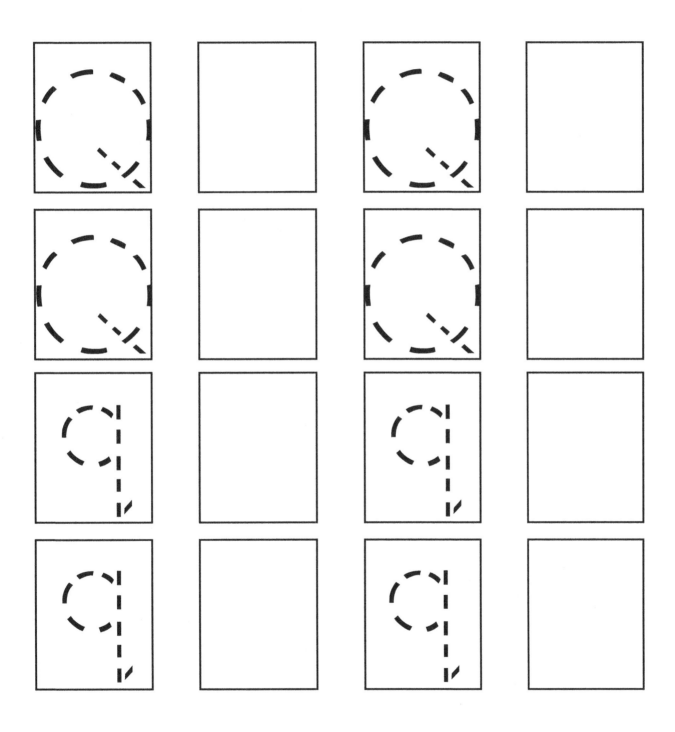

Rr

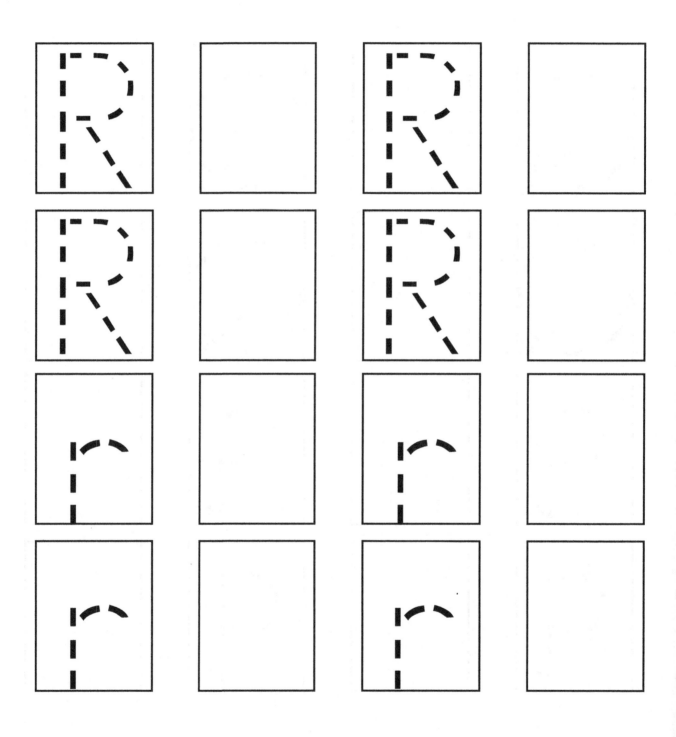

Ss

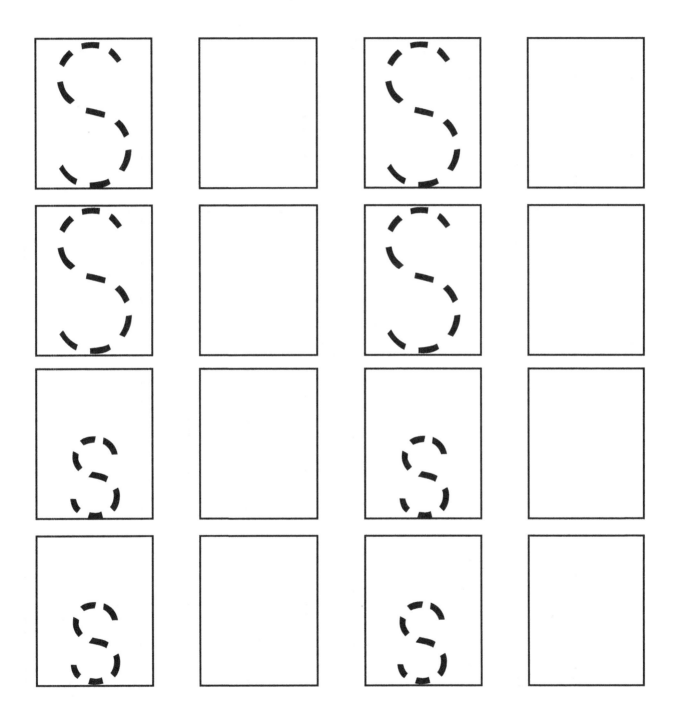

T t

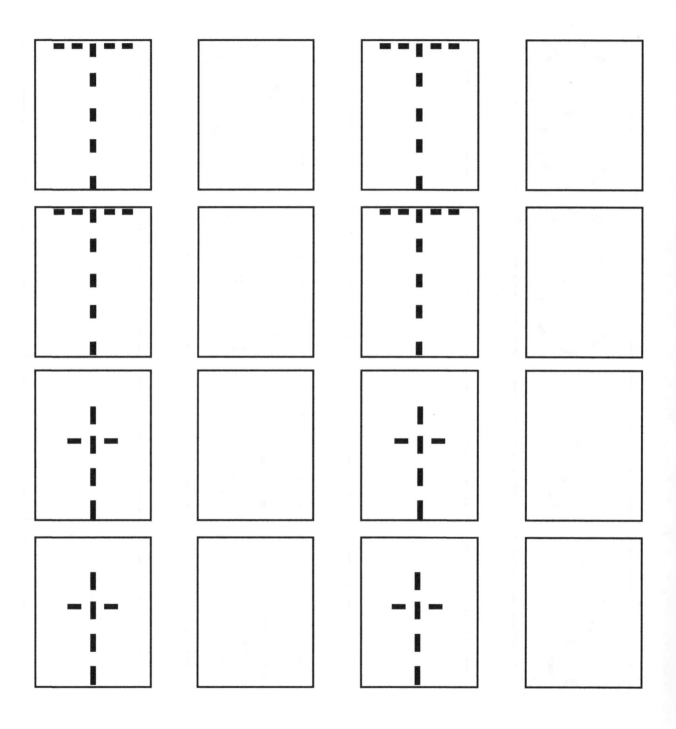

Uu

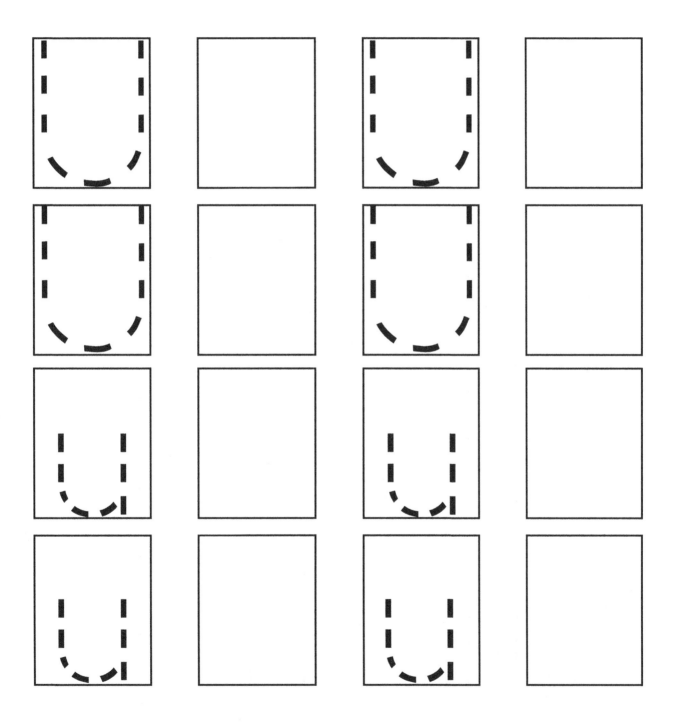

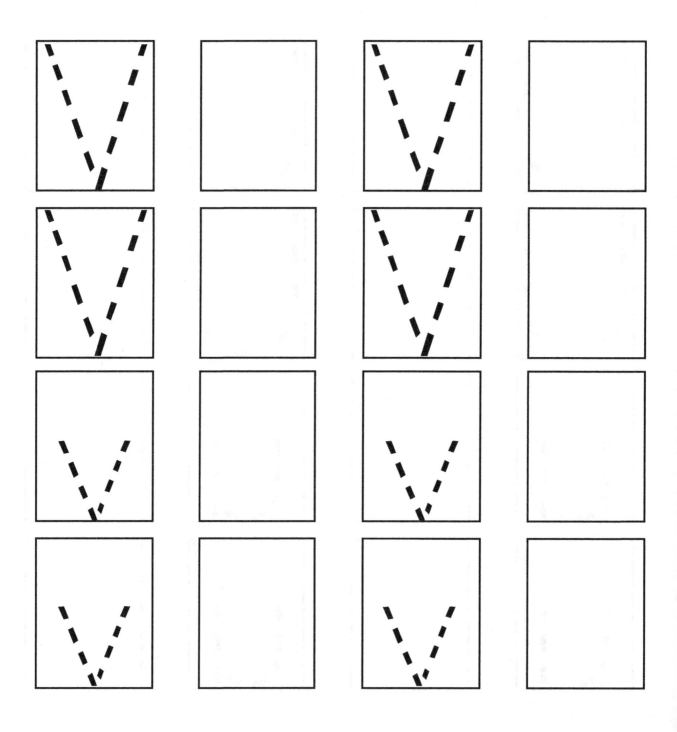

Ww

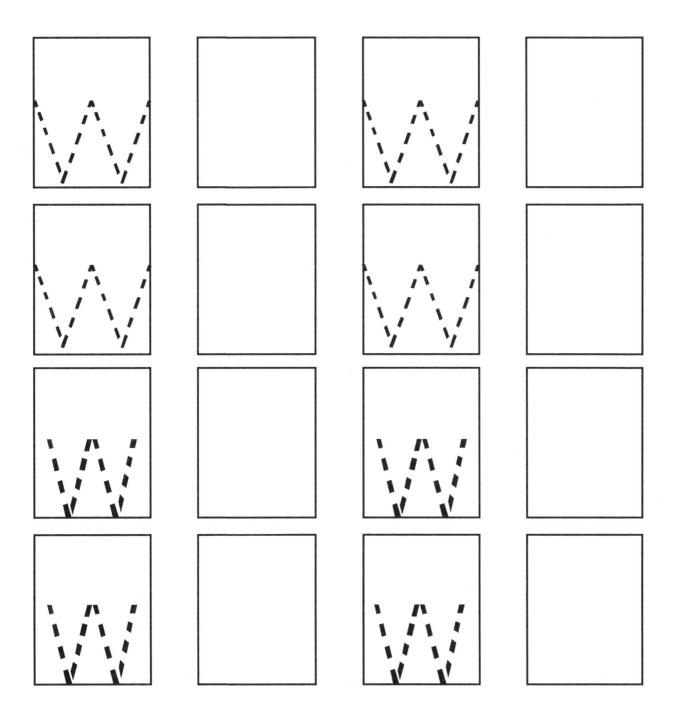

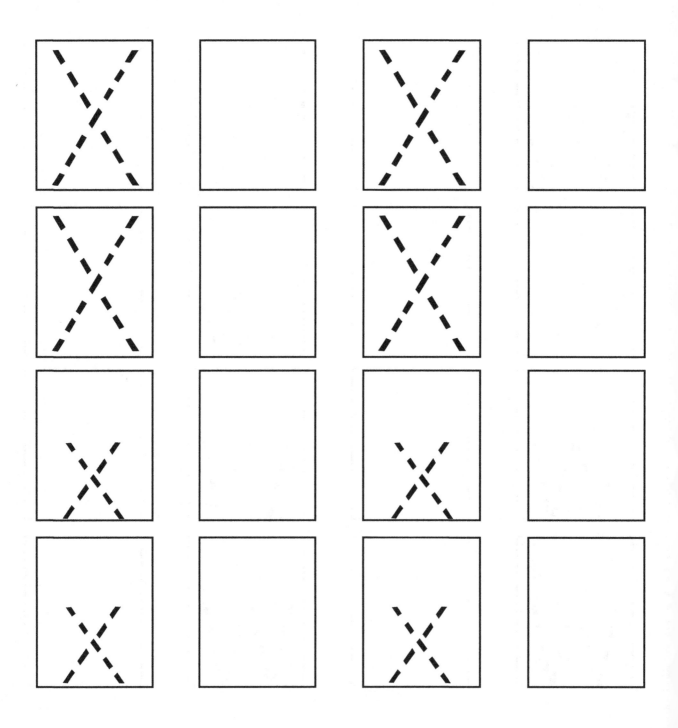

Yy

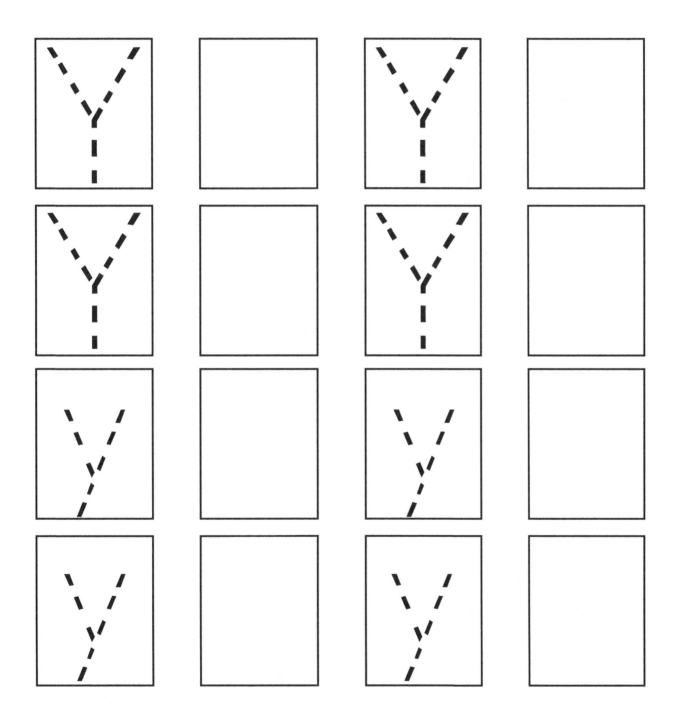

63

Zz

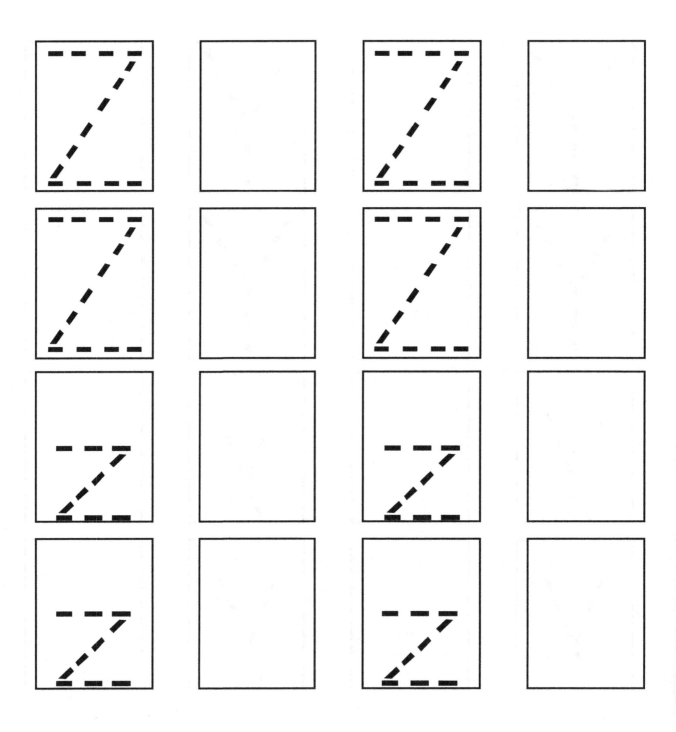

O

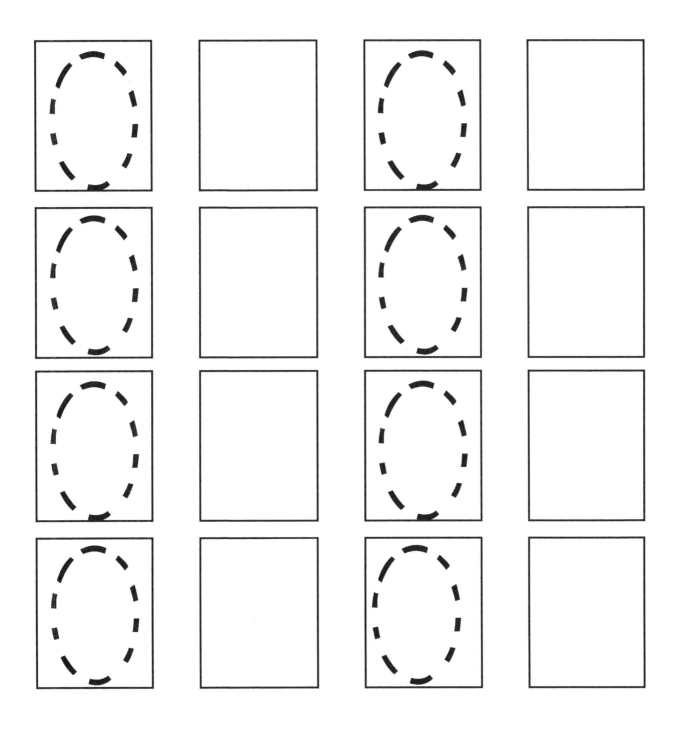

1

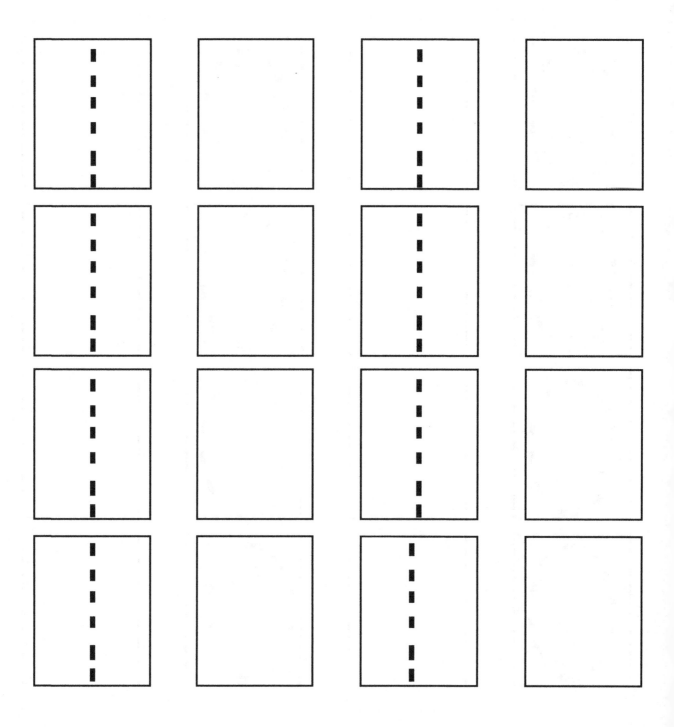

2

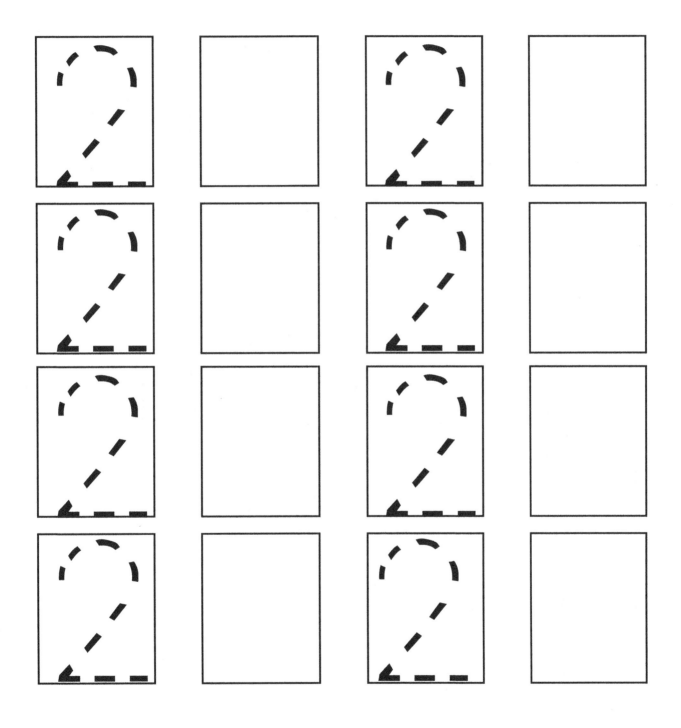

3

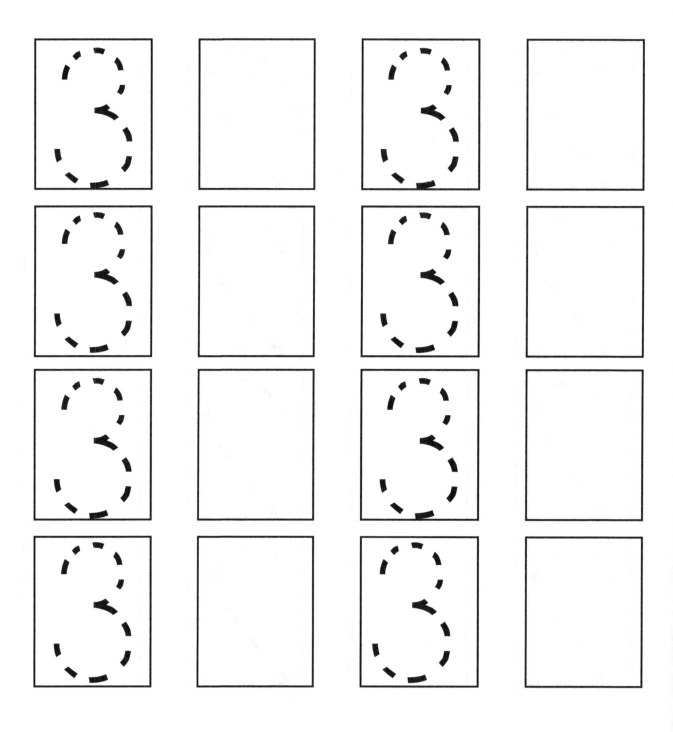

4

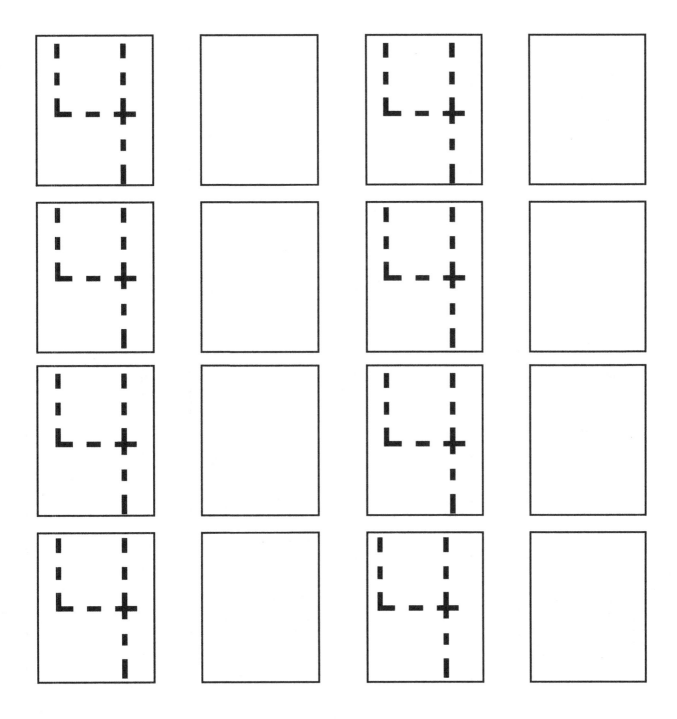

5

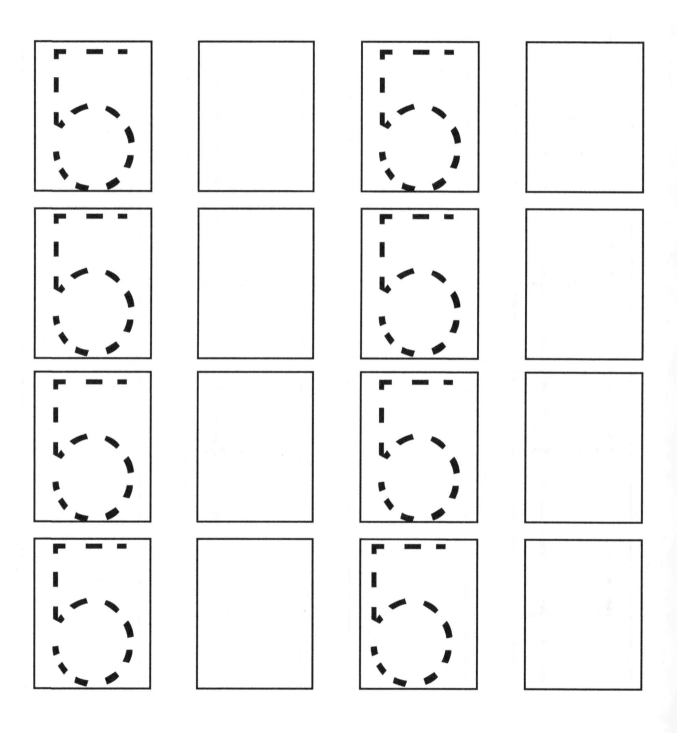

6

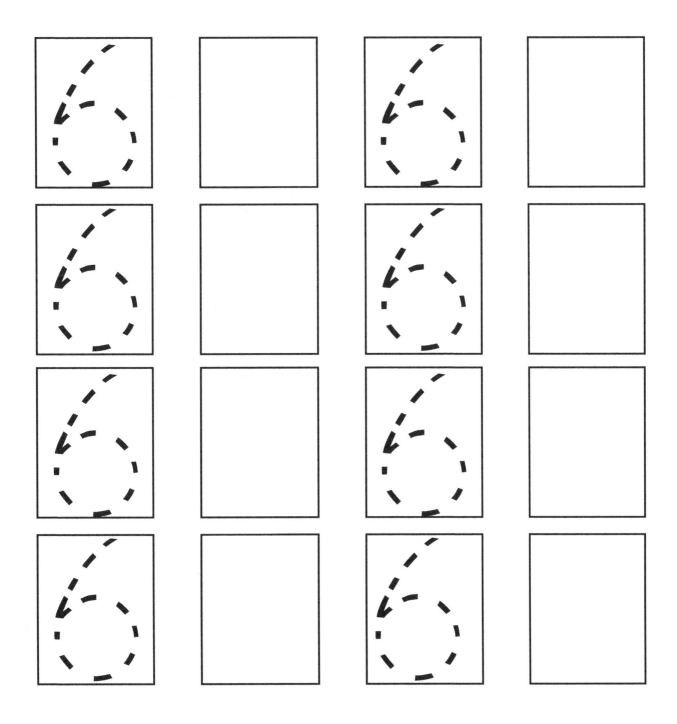

7

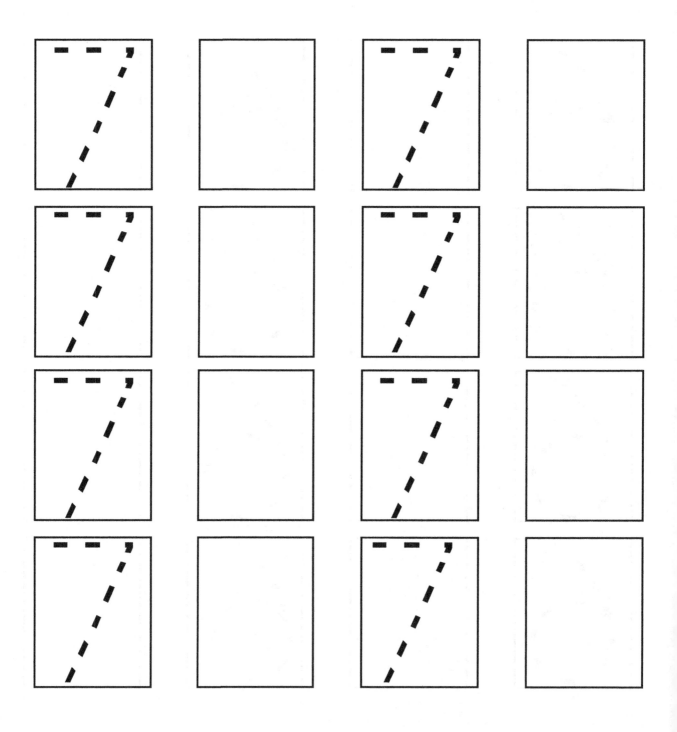

8

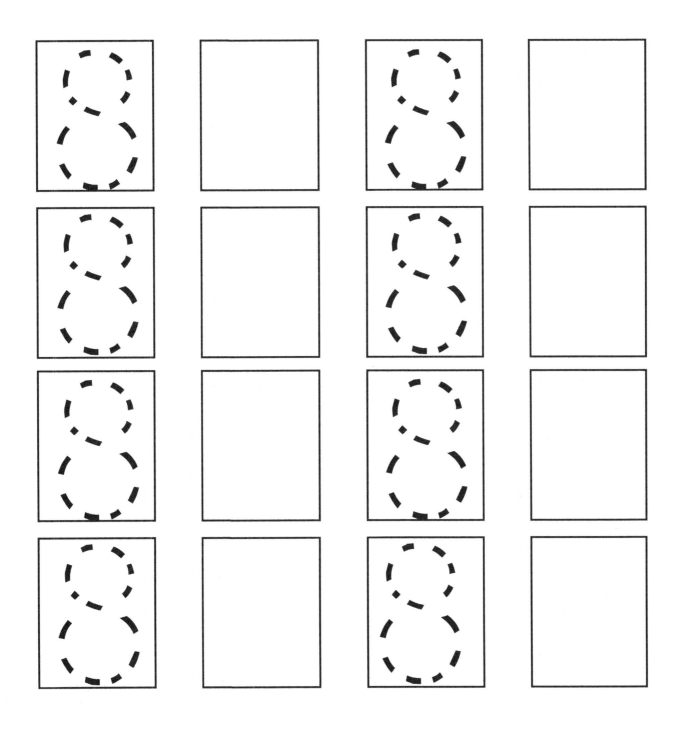

9

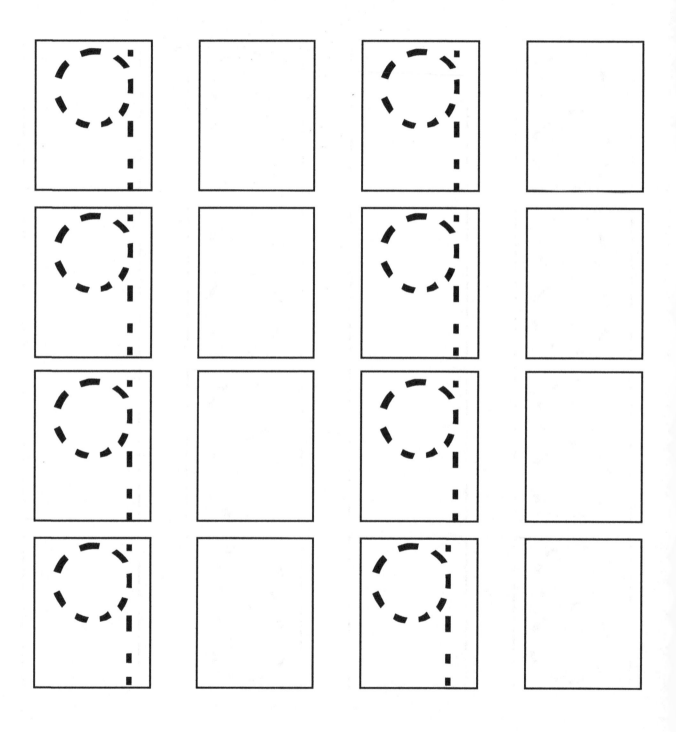

10

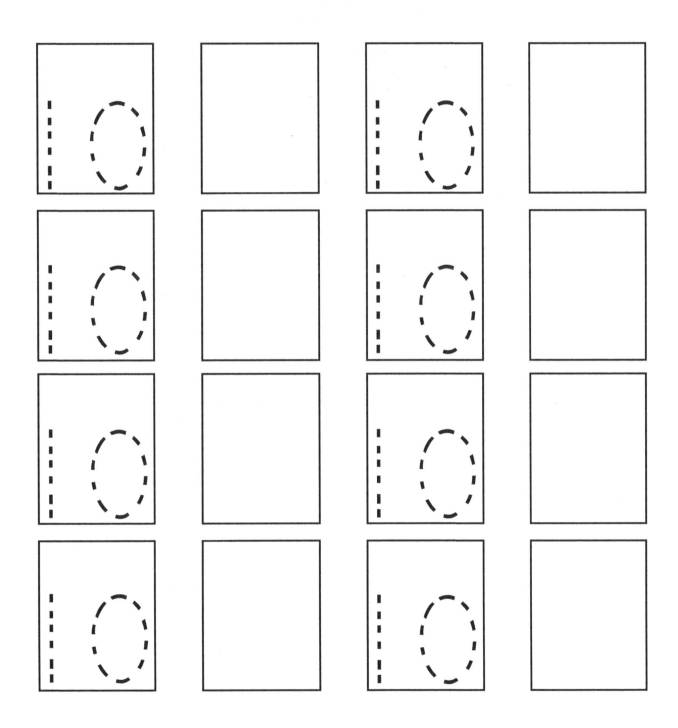

Color the pictures that start with letter at the top

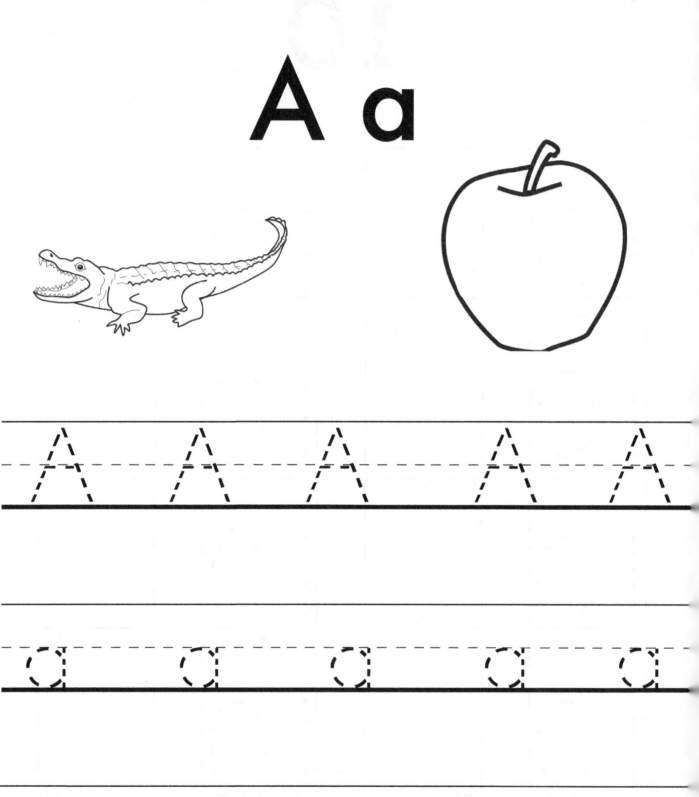

A a

Color the pictures that start with letter at the top

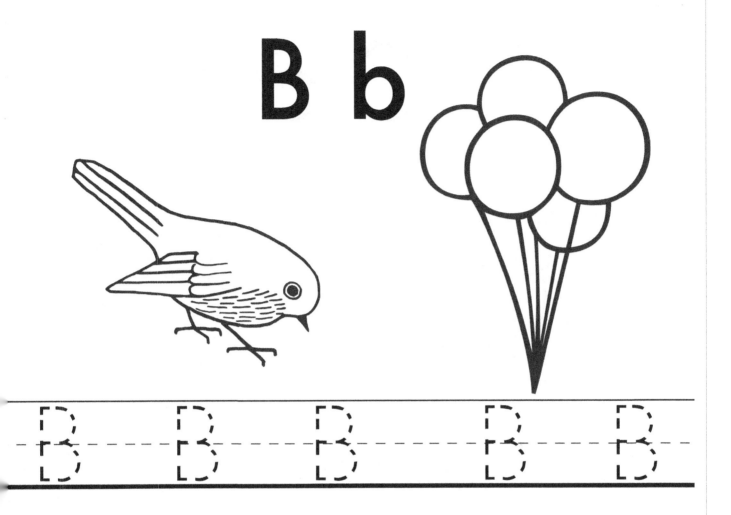

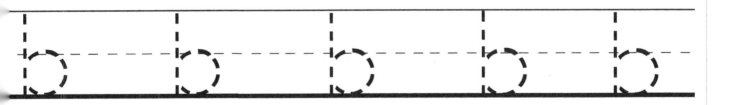

Color the pictures that start with letter at the top

C c

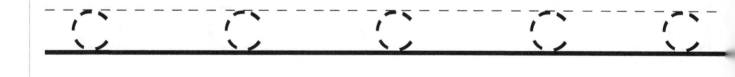

Color the pictures that start with letter at the top

D d

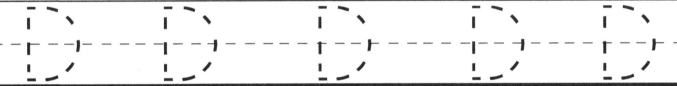

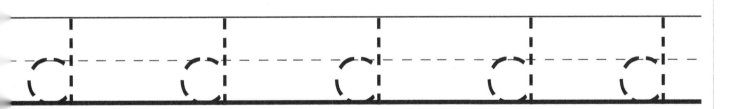

Color the pictures that start with letter at the top

E e

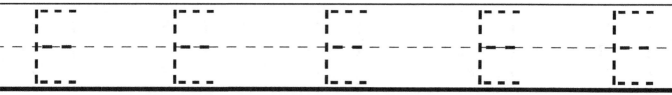

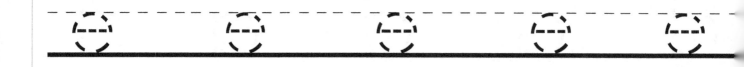

Color the pictures that start with letter at the top

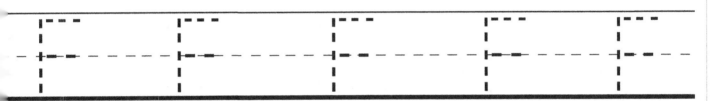

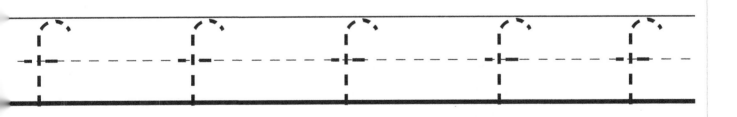

Color the pictures that start with letter at the top

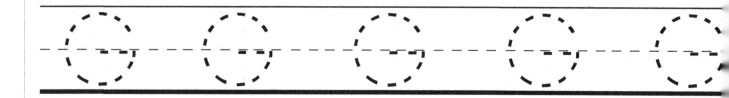

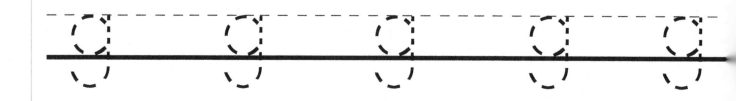

Color the pictures that start with letter at the top

H h

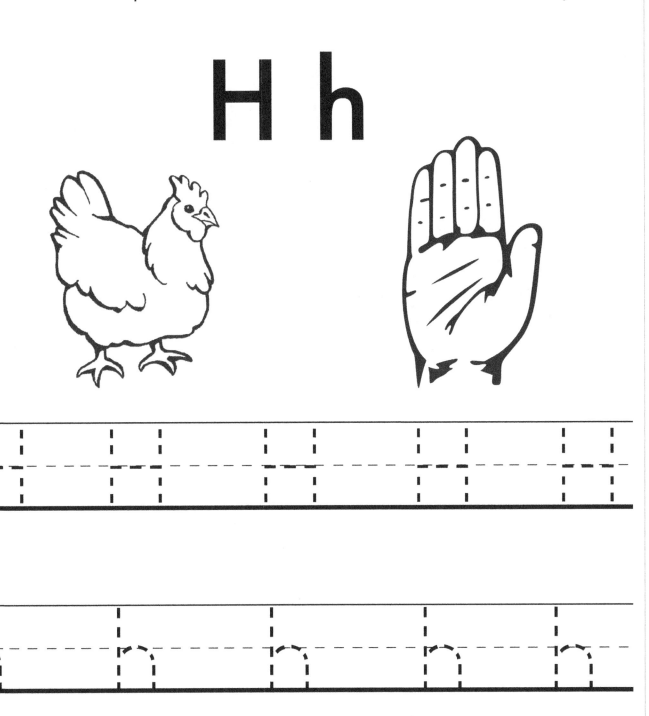

Color the pictures that start with letter at the top

I i

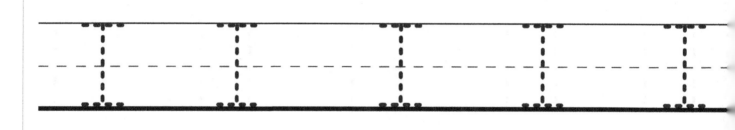

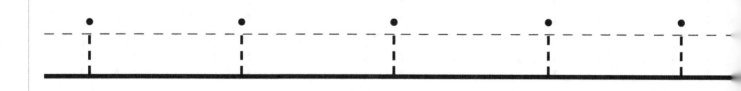

84

Color the pictures that start with letter at the top

J j

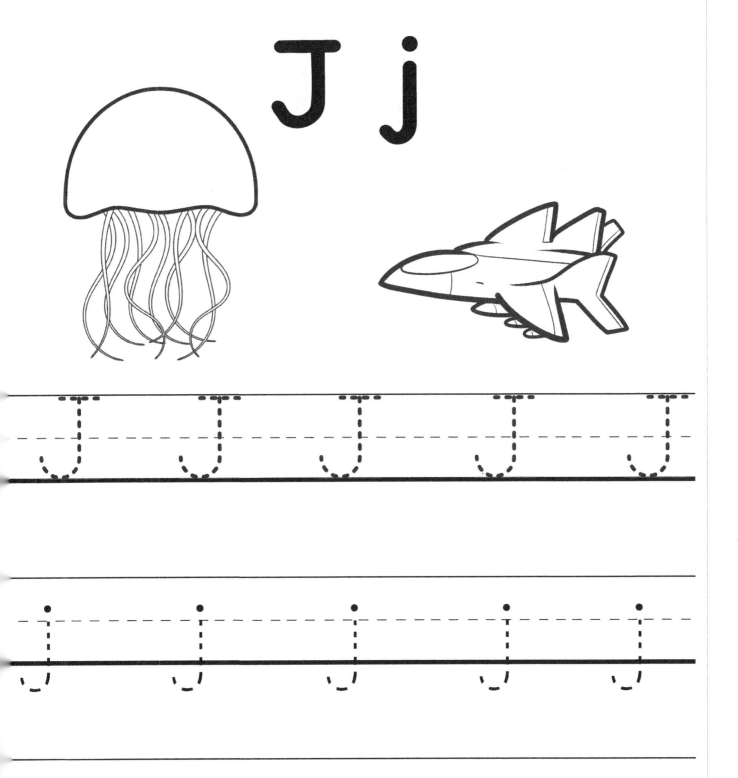

Color the pictures that start with letter at the top

K k

Color the pictures that start with letter at the top

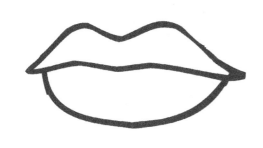

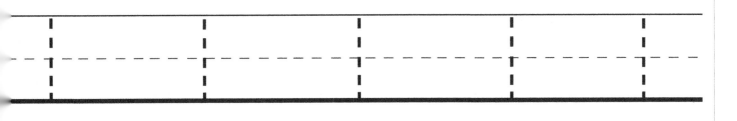

Color the pictures that start with letter at the top

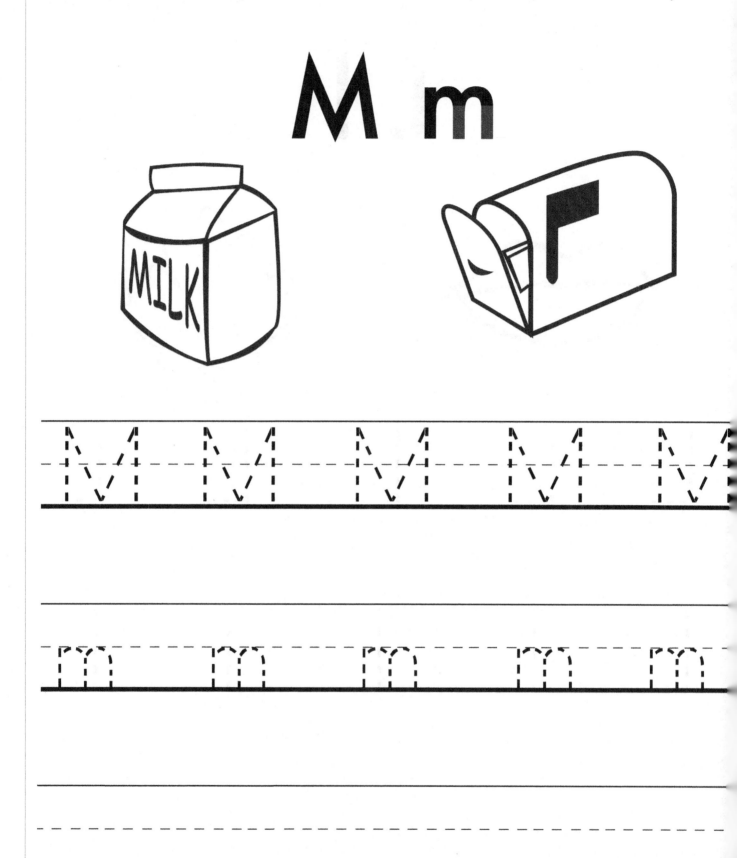

Color the pictures that start with letter at the top

N n

Color the pictures that start with letter at the top

9

Color the pictures that start with letter at the top

P p

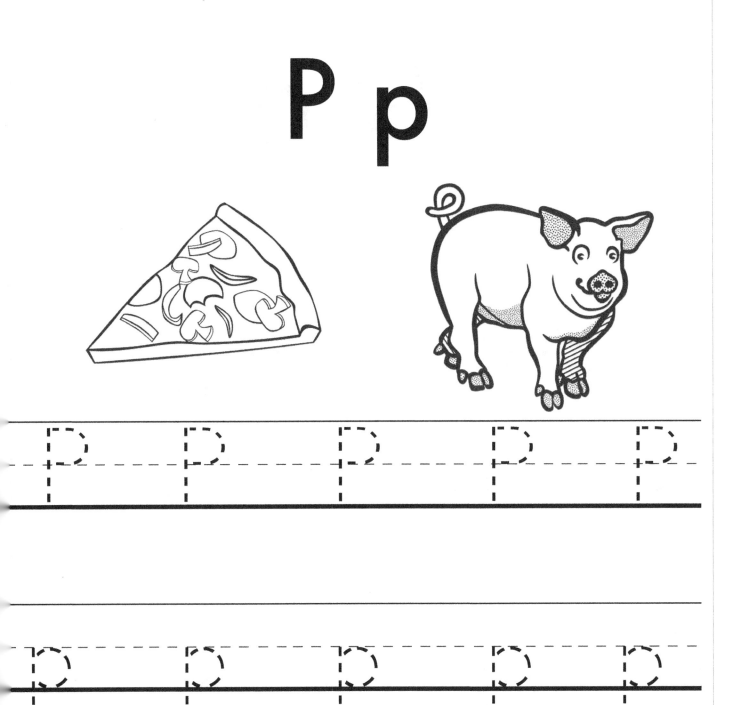

Color the pictures that start with letter at the top

Q q

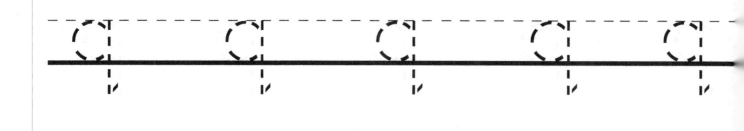

Color the pictures that start with letter at the top

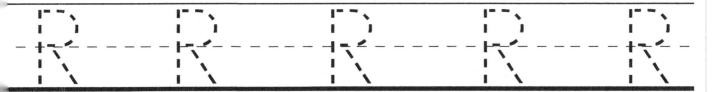

Color the pictures that start with letter at the top

Color the pictures that start with letter at the top

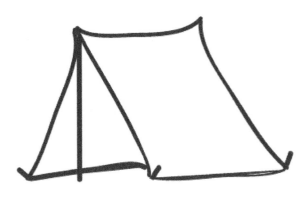

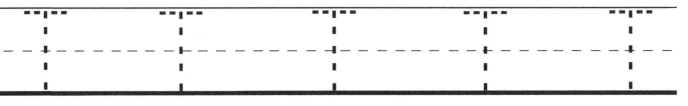

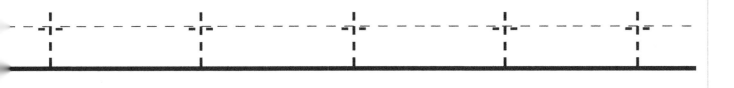

Color the pictures that start with letter at the top

Color the pictures that start with letter at the top

V v

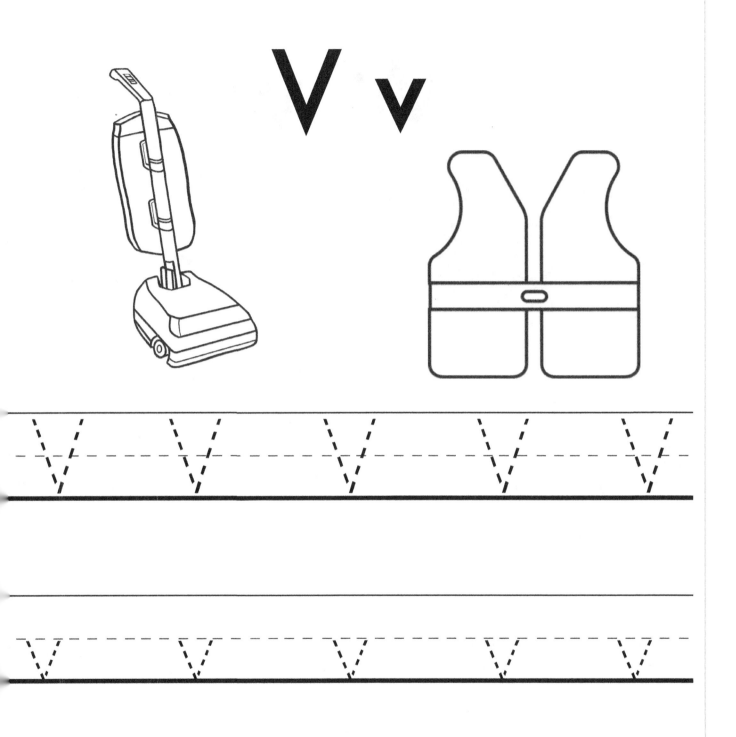

Color the pictures that start with letter at the top

W w

Color the pictures and trace the letters

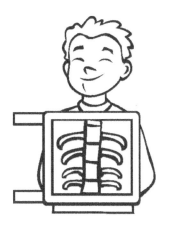

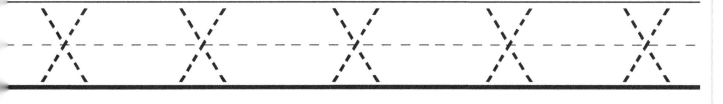

Color the pictures and trace the letters

Y y

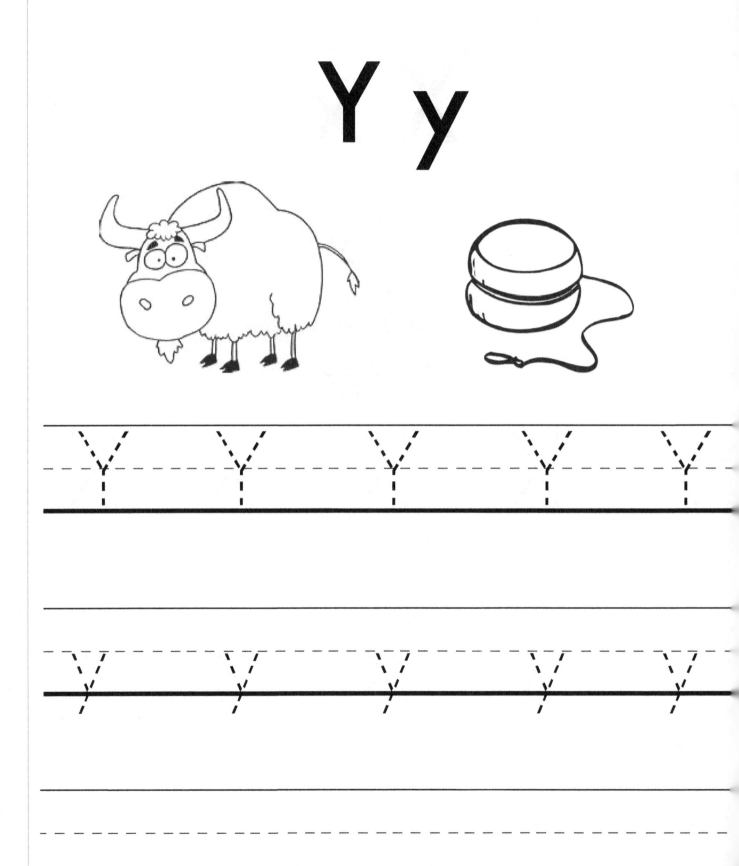

Color the pictures and trace the letters

Z z

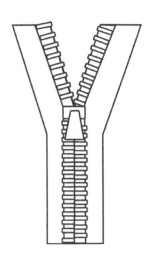

Z Z Z Z Z

Z Z Z Z Z

O

1

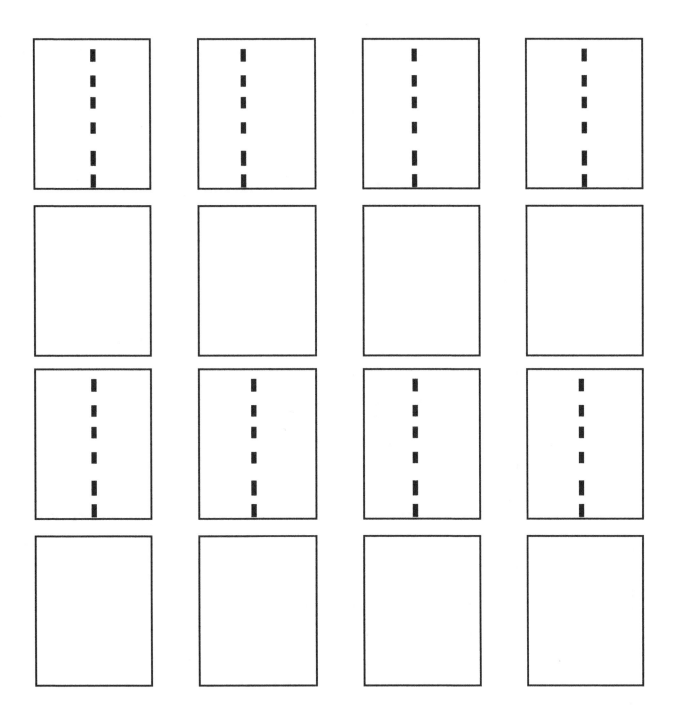

2

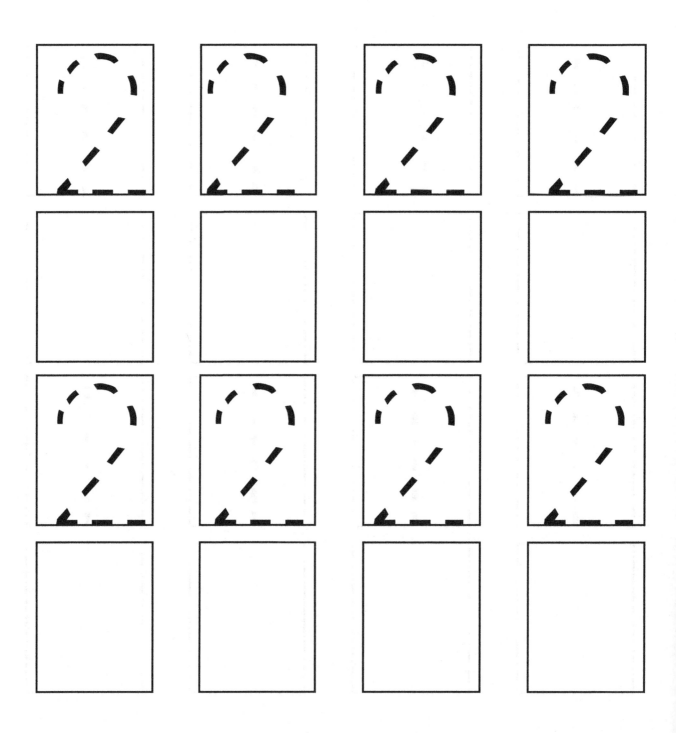

3

4

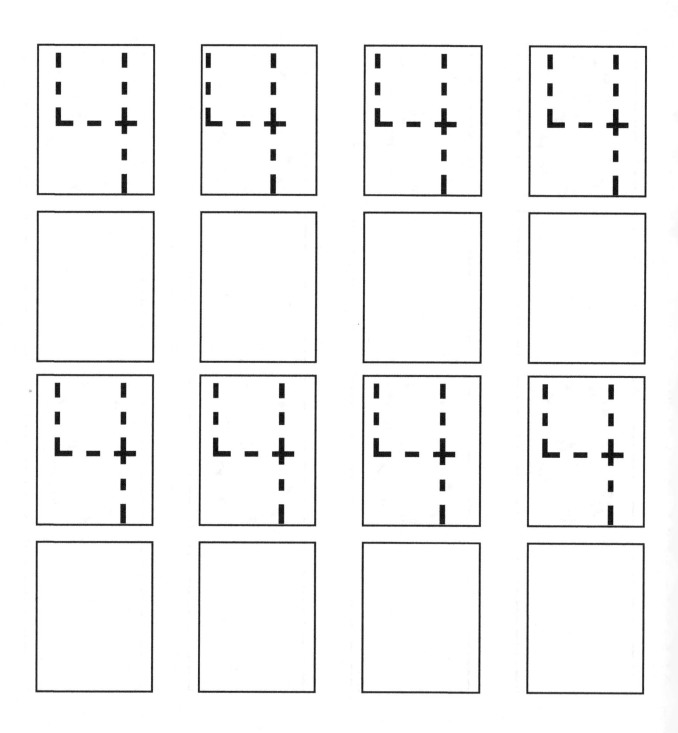

10

5

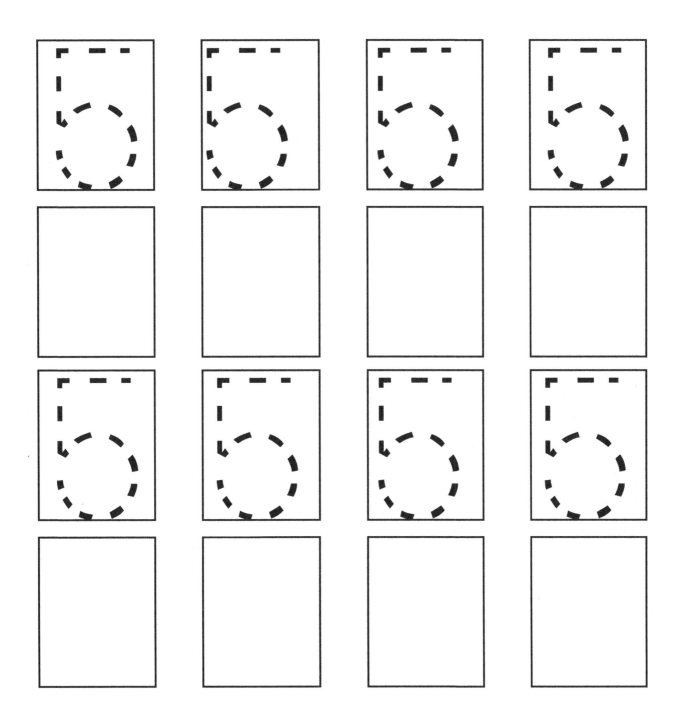

6

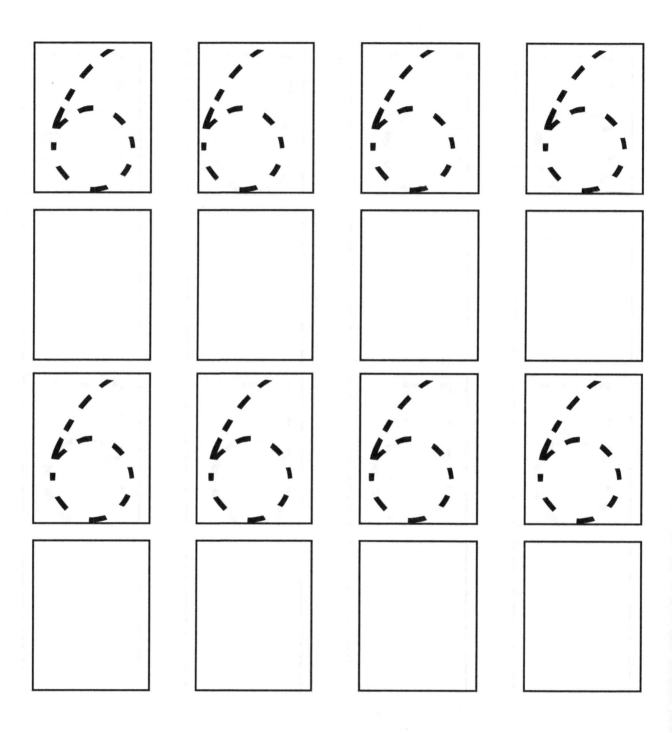

7

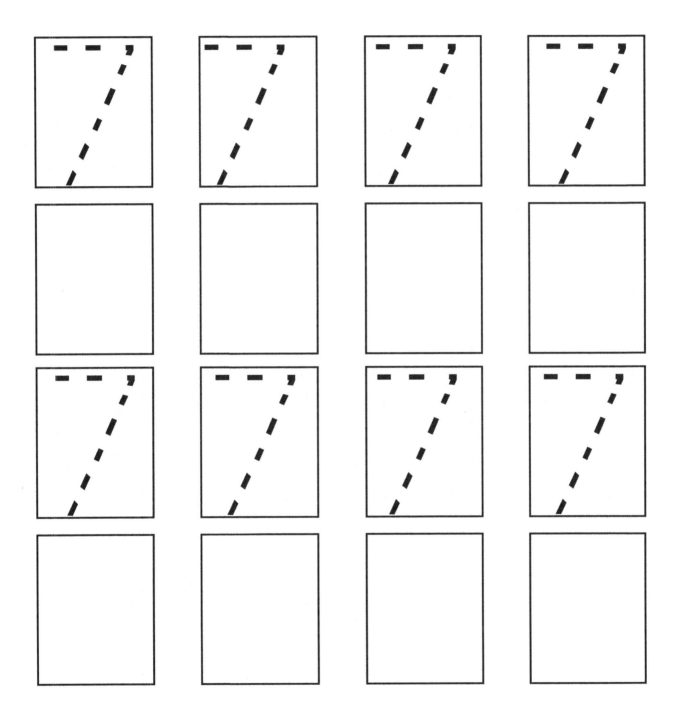

8

9

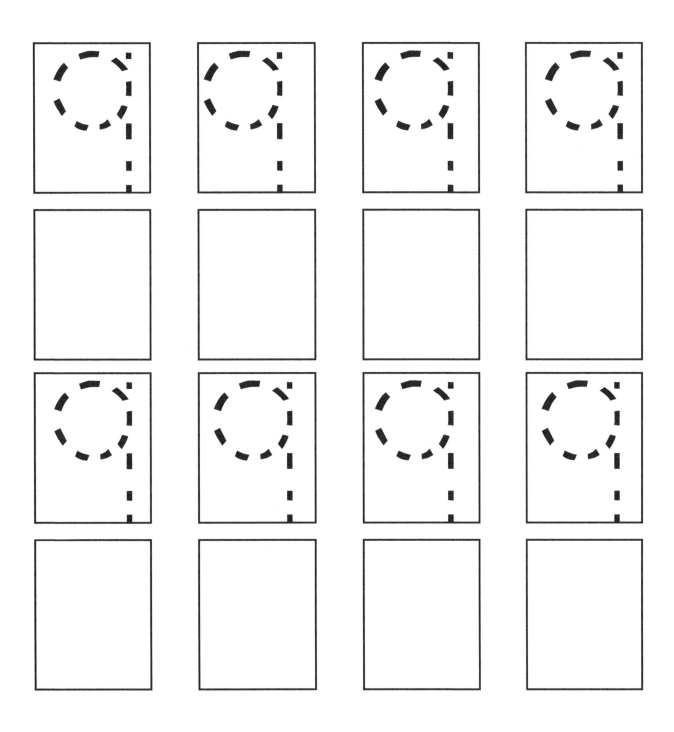

10

Made in the USA
Monee, IL
25 October 2024

68656310R00063